THE ENLIGHTENED
CAPITALISM MANIFESTO
A Blueprint for a Revitalized America

THE ENLIGHTENED
CAPITALISM MANIFESTO
A Blueprint for a Revitalized America

By

HENRY B. ZIMMER

First Edition
Trade paperback ISBN: 978-0-615-90479-5

Website: www.enlightenedcapitalism.us

Cover design by Elijah Toten
Website created by Courtney Eaves

This book is dedicated to my wife and editor Loretta Vlach who provided loving encouragement and support

The Enlightened Capitalism Manifesto

CONTENTS

INTRODUCTION

In 2012, President Barack Obama, campaigning for a second term in office, made a general appeal requesting proposals for "change". Taking him at his word, I composed a twenty-page letter that I mailed to him around the time of his inauguration in January 2013. I made a number of concrete recommendations covering many areas where I believe major reform is required. All I received was a form letter from The White House six months later touting the accomplishments of Mr. Obama's administration to date. Perhaps the reason is because I left out the "c" in Barack when I addressed my correspondence and Microsoft Word's spell check didn't catch my mistake.

When Mr. Obama took office, the economy was mired in a cesspool. Of course, economic conditions always fluctuate from time to time. No doubt, there has been some recovery. Mr. Obama's letter states that six million jobs have been created during his administration, but he doesn't mention the fact that most of these jobs had been lost in the first place around the time he came to office. Current "real" rates of unemployment are unacceptable. He referred to the statistic that we now buy more American cars than we have in five years and less foreign oil than we have in twenty. Well, six years ago, no one was buying cars at all–foreign or domestic- and when manufacturing is down, there is less demand for oil.

In July 2013, the City of Detroit filed for bankruptcy. A recent MarketWatch article, mentioned that, in the state of Nevada, the total worth of homes is less than the amount currently owed on these homes.

I'm not necessarily criticizing the current administration. I believe that most of our economic problems originated under his predecessor's watch. America badly needs a new approach and that is the reason for this book.

Of course, you might ask, "Who is Henry Zimmer, and what can he possibly have to say?" I am a semi-retired CPA living in Palm Desert California. Although I am a U.S. citizen, I've lived most of my life in Canada where I hold a Chartered Accountant (CA) designation. My undergraduate degree was in English. My business career has spanned the last half-century during which I wrote 15 books on Canadian taxation and financial planning, several of which were best sellers. At the moment, I am virtually unknown in the United States. I keep myself occupied by training Canadian Chartered Accountants who would like to obtain a U.S. CPA designation.

Back in 1984, I joined forces with a 17-year-old computer genius and we developed what became Canada's foremost income tax software. Intuit, which operates Turbo Tax and Quicken, owns my former business today.

In 1991, my partner and I sold our company and I was able to retire. My last book on financial planning was written in 1993. Until recently, I never thought that I would have anything more to say. Although I'm not a social butterfly, I was reasonably well connected in "the day". I was listed in Canadian Who's Who and was on a first-name basis with two Canadian Prime Ministers.

Over the past twenty years, I've watched the world go by and I've witnessed an alarming general deterioration of many of the world's economies and the polarization of political ideologies. **All this has happened while technological advances have been simply mind-boggling**. I still remember seeing my first desktop Xerox copier in 1964. Now, the Internet connects me to the world and I can access it on my iPad with a few touches of my fingertips!

While I will refer to world economies and political systems from time to time in this book, I will confine my recommendations for changes to the United States only **No one can "fix" the whole world**. I believe, however, that there are many improvements that can be made to solve virtually all our U.S. *domestic* problems**. I am a firm believer that charity begins at home.** If you want to send aid to starving children in Africa, bring lasting peace to the Middle East or force China to institute recycling policies, you have my blessings. But that's not what this book is all about.

My premise is that Unbridled Capitalism (as we know it in the U.S.) is *obsolete* and that our political

system is broken as a result of corruption and the polarization of our major political parties.

I believe that embracing the **Doctrine of Enlightened Capitalism** will solve most of our problems and restore the United States to its former greatness.

In just a few words, the adoption of a framework of Enlightened Capitalism requires adherence to the concept of **social responsibility** because a system that embraces social responsibility does not just favor the very wealthy or the nation's political leaders. *An effective capitalistic system requires the participation of <u>every American</u> who believes he or she is a stakeholder in setting the future course of our country.*

Until recently, I believed that I had coined the term "Enlightened Capitalism. I've been using it for several years in my lectures. When I began to do a bit of research, I found that others have come before me. (New inventions and ideas can rarely be attributed to a single person.) However, although my concept of social responsibility is not original, *I don't believe anyone else has attempted to compile an **integrated system of economic and political reforms to implement the Doctrine of Enlightened Capitalism.*** Many of my recommendations for change require the kind of thinking that is often referred to these days as coming from "outside the box". It is very easy to criticize and complain about what's wrong with this, that or the other system. However, *unless someone offers viable alternatives to build on, nothing constructive will happen.*

I have organized this material to be **interactive with you, the reader**. I have designed a simple website at www.enlightenedcapitalism.us . As I propose specific changes to our economic and political systems, I will, of course present my reasoning. *At the conclusion of each chapter, I will ask one or more questions designed to elicit yes, no or undecided votes from* **you**. At the end of the book, there is a complete list of all the questions. There is also a pdf. on the website that will let you print out the questions as a single document so that you can keep track of your responses chapter-by-chapter. *When you have finished reading the entire book, you will be asked to input a password and you may then cast your vote on each of my proposals, one after another.*

When you have answered all the questions online, you may then press a "submit" button and your answers will be integrated into the totals. By logging on to the website, you will be able to view the total number of votes and percentages as they change from time-to time. I only ask that you refrain from voting multiple times. You will be able to gauge the opinions of your fellow Americans on a great variety of issues. *You will also be able to post comments on any of the questions by logging on with your email address. I promise not to share this address with anyone.*

My objective is to contact the business, economic and political press with a view towards obtaining ever-growing grass roots participation. **It is only by dispelling apathy and lethargy that meaningful reform is possible.**

I will endeavor to present all my material in simple easy-to-follow language that you will be able to follow effortlessly. I will use only two graphs and very few numbers. I strongly encourage you to read *every chapter,* even if you don't think that certain topics are relevant to you. There are certain concepts that you owe it to yourself to understand if you are to survive, let alone prosper, in these volatile times.

One final point. At the present time, this book is available in electronic format and is self-published as a trade paperback through Create Space. I believe that the prevalence of printed books will decline greatly over time. However, printed books are still very mainstream. I really don't want to spend a year or two submitting this manuscript to various publishing houses in the hope of enticing a mainstream publisher to print and distribute it. *The time for reform is now*! If you find this book informative and useful and you have contacts within the publishing industry, please pass this message on. I can be reached by email at henry@enlightenedcapitalism.us or cpa-now@dc.rr.com. Hopefully, I will soon be able to remove this last paragraph from my introduction.

Question 1: **Do you believe our top priority as Americans is to clean up our own economic and political house?**

Yes___ No___ Undecided___

CHAPTER 1
THE EQUALITY MYTH

*"We hold these truths to be self-evident that **all men are created equal**..."*
Declaration of Independence, 1776

When Thomas Jefferson penned these words, his intent was to renounce the concept of the divine right of kings. I don't think there are too many Americans who would argue against giving everyone the same rights and responsibilities under the law, regardless of religion, race or creed. In these respects, we are all equal.

On the other hand, at the risk of being politically incorrect, I submit that we are not all created equal *when it comes to our diverse aptitudes and abilities.* Some of us are superb athletes, while others are mechanically inclined or technologically savvy. There are those of us who have well-developed people skills and better-than-average abilities to communicate. These traits are found in our salespeople and teachers. There are leaders and followers. I don't believe that our society could function without those millions of Americans who simply want a steady job within a structured environment, a paycheck adequate to meet their expenses and sufficient leisure time to enjoy family, friends and various hobbies and activities.

Then there are those whose aptitudes lead to careers in making or managing investments, overseeing manufacturing, wholesale or retail businesses, resource development, technology, real estate, and banking. These are the people who, by their very natures, are willing to accept varying levels of risk in exchange for the expectation of greater rewards. The rewards are often measured in terms of monetary wealth, but they also bring the satisfaction of having created a new structure, such as an attractive housing development, a new business enterprise or innovative technology. After a certain point, wealth accumulation often becomes nothing more than keeping score of one's relative successes measured against his or her peers. **By definition, the people I've described in this paragraph comprise our nation's Capitalists**

While their motivations might be primarily *self-serving*, the Capitalists are the ones who foster America's economic growth by employing millions of their fellow citizens. In the last sentence, I used the words "self-serving". Please don't misunderstand. I certainly am **not** advocating that our nation should adopt Communism as a way of life. **Under Communism, the state owns everything and everyone works for the state.** Most of the world learned in 1989-91 that Communism does not work. To excel, or to be even mildly productive, almost of us require **incentives**. These include monetary compensation and job satisfaction. *Communism is not a system that provides sufficient incentives and rewards to* *ensure a thriving economy.*

Of course Capitalists are self-serving. They are generally motivated primarily by a desire for monetary compensation for themselves and their families. I believe these people are entitled to a ***reasonably* enhanced standard of living** as a reward for their accomplishments (although what constitutes reasonable is subject to debate). In this context, I don't think of the word "self-serving" as having a negative connotation. Furthermore, any American who has the aptitude and desire (and often a great deal of luck) can join the ranks of the Capitalists. There is no caste system in this country to hold anyone back.

My thesis is simply that <u>Unbridled</u> Capitalism must be reined in before our society collapses entirely. The self-serving interests of our nation's Capitalists, present and future, must be tempered with *social responsibility*. This is the essence of <u>Enlightened</u> Capitalism. We need to set broad guidelines for what is a reasonable standard of reward for our nation's Capitalists so that our country's *overall* prosperity can be enhanced.

I believe that an economic and political system that embraces the concept of Enlightened Capitalism **requires the cooperation and participation of *all* Americans to succeed. *We cannot expect the rich to carry the poor on their backs indefinitely.*** An article in Financialsamuri.com that I will discuss in detail later, reveals that the **bottom 50% of all taxpayers now contributes less than 3% of total U.S. tax revenues.** This inequity must be rectified, but **NOT** by taxing the "poor". Rather, our economic and social framework must be modified to provide the training and jobs necessary to reduce the number of people living below the poverty line. The goal should be to involve virtually all Americans in sharing our country's tax burden, each according to their means. *Today's bottom 50% must become willing and able tax**payers**.*

At this point, you may be asking yourself "what is the difference between Enlightened Capitalism and Socialism? Somewhat facetiously, I suggest that there is little or no difference! **Both advocate private enterprise tempered by social responsibility.** *Neither should be confused with Communism.*

For a very long time, Americans considered Communism Public Enemy #1. (Today, our main enemy is terrorism, but that's another issue.) **Unfortunately, the terms "Communism" and "Socialism" have become mistakenly considered by many Americans to be interchangeable.** Communism embraces the philosophy that all major enterprise should be *state-owned*. To repeat what I said before, **Socialism does *not* advocate government control of business. It merely imposes a regime of social responsibility on everyone- each according to their abilities to contribute. The two terms are not at all synonymous.**

I have lived most of my life in Canada and am a citizen of both Canada and the U.S. On many occasions, I have seen Americans expressing disdain for Canadians with words like, "You guys are all Socialists." They have heard that Canada has "socialized medicine" and jump to the erroneous conclusion that the State runs everything. This is not the case at all. It is true that the Government of Canada controls the nation's healthcare system, but, as I will show you later, the Canadian healthcare system works very well. Outside of socialized medicine, Canadian private enterprise is essentially left to function with the same freedoms that are enjoyed in the United States.

Unfortunately, the stigma of the word "Socialism" negates the possibility that any meaningful reforms can be implemented in the United States under any banner that incorporates that word. **Hence the need for another term, and "Enlightened Capitalism" is, in my opinion, an excellent choice.**

I reiterate my thesis that Unbridled Capitalism must be stopped before our economy and the American way of life disintegrates completely. This is because **Unbridled Capitalism creates a totally unacceptable concentration of wealth in the hands of an elite few.**

While I repeat that I have no issue with the concept of permitting entrepreneurs and innovators from amassing personal wealth, I believe they owe it to the American people to pass on a bigger slice of the pie than is now the case.

The numbers below, compiled from information provided by the U.S. Census, Spectrem Research and Forbes Magazine, paint a chilling picture:

Approximate population of the United States - 314 Million

Approximate number of households (Average 2.6 persons per) - **117 Million**

Number of households with a net worth of $1Million or more* - 9 Million

Number of households with a net worth of $5 Million

or more* - 1.4 Million

Number of households with a net worth of $25Million or more* - 100,000

* (Excluding the value of a primary residence)

Number of American Billionaires - 442

These numbers reveal that the wealth of this nation is controlled by about 1% of its citizens.

As you might expect, a certain percentage of the multi-millionaire households includes athletes and entertainers as well as those who have inherited their wealth and may take little or no interest in how the country is run. It would also be unfair to ignore the philanthropic contributions that these households make and the fact that they bear the lion's share of the total tax burden. (More about that later.)

Nevertheless, I don't believe that the interests of the 1% who are multi-millionaires and the interests of the other 99% of all Americans are even remotely the same, at least from an *economic or political* **perspective.** Most Americans, rich and poor, are aligned with either the Democratic or Republican parties, but *who is providing the funds to elect our political leaders and whose interests do these elected politicians support?* While it is true that we all consider ourselves to be patriotic Americans, again, in no way are the two groups on the same page in most other respects.

In the introduction to this book, I emphasized the need for change. **If meaningful change is to happen, the impetus must emanate from a** *grass roots* **movement that will reform our political system so that it represents**

fairly the needs of the majority of Americans.

As a nation, our biggest enemy is apathy. I don't see any meaningful help coming from the existing cadre of politicians- Republican or Democrat. Meaningful reforms call for a new brand of political leaders who will champion them through the system and make them happen.

Before moving on to an analysis of why Capitalism, as we know it, has failed the American people, I think you may find it interesting to read a short analysis of the composition of our U.S. Billionaires that appeared a recent article on Forbes.com:

Number of Billionaires created by:

Investment - 102

Financing - 21

Technology - 53

Energy - 33

Food and beverage - 33

Media - 34

Other - 166

Many of those who are included in the "other" category are those who have inherited their wealth, such as members of Sam Walton's (Walmart) family. My instincts tell me that the *multi-millionaires* are and will be more resistant to economic and political reform than the *billionaires*. I believe that many of the billionaires are no longer motivated by wealth creation. As a group, they also comprise our nation's largest philanthropists.

I should like to mention at this point that, *nowhere* within my proposals for the implementation of Enlightened Capitalism, do I advocate the confiscation of wealth accumulated to date by anyone. This will become clearer as you examine my specific recommendations.

Now, on to one of the main reasons why I believe Capitalism has failed us. I may be oversimplifying, but I believe that my broad brushstrokes present a reasonably accurate picture. Before 1981, top marginal federal income tax rates were imposed in the U.S. at 70%. When Ronald Reagan assumed the presidency, his advisors prevailed upon him to lower the top rate to 50%. The thinking was that high tax rates severely curtail the willingness of the country's "movers and shakers" to take business risks. A policy of lowering tax rates was therefore designed to provide greater incentive to expand businesses, start new ones, and **create employment**. The loss of tax revenues from the wealthy was expected to be more than offset by additional taxes derived from increasing the employment *base*. As more Americans prospered, the increase in their disposable incomes was anticipated to lead to more spending and further job creation.

This theory, which became known as the "trickle-down effect", postulated that wealth would *flow downwards* from the rich to the middle and lower classes, thereby increasing overall prosperity. The media gave this economic model the name "Reaganomics". In 1986, the

50% top rate was lowered to only 28%.

Conceptually, I believe that Reaganomics made a great deal of sense and that the incentives of low taxation, *if properly applied* might have heralded a long-lasting triumph of the Capitalist economic model.

Unfortunately, President Reagan's advisors overlooked two very important factors. The first was greed-*im*pure and simple; and the second was the burgeoning technological revolution that gradually facilitated globalization.

Once Reaganomics was introduced, the captains of industry quickly realized that they could magnify their profits exponentially by moving jobs to third-world countries where labor costs were significantly lower. As technological advances created instantaneous global communications, the "movers and shakers" then hired spin-doctors to advance the concept of "globalization", promoting the concept that America would play a major role in helping under-developed counties move into the 20th and 21st centuries. **They intentionally underplayed the staggering loss of domestic jobs and the destruction of America's middle class.** Our elected representatives enthusiastically bought into the program. They now had a good reason to travel internationally at taxpayer expense.

A March 2012 publication sponsored by the Information Technology and Innovation Foundation reveals that, from 2000-2010, the U.S. lost 5.7 million manufacturing jobs which can be translated into one-third of all manufacturing jobs. Although one might have expected technology to have picked up the slack, this has not been the case.

Although technological inventions, such as the iPad are designed in the U.S., they are manufactured and assembled in China and other countries. Much of the telephone support activities provided by American companies is outsourced to other countries such as India and the Philippines.

Beyond a few protests and some grumbling, Americans have passively accepted the losses in jobs. Much of the job creation that has occurred in the last decade has been restricted to low-paying positions in the hospitality industry. These are often referred to as "McJobs". In the meantime, skilled labor has been shunted over to the sidelines and there have been few government-sponsored retraining programs.

Our greatest enemies continue to be apathy and complacency. Instead of actively pursuing change, we sit in front of our television sets and channel our collective focus on the lives and doings of actors and athletes. Sure, everyone enjoys being entertained. But why should you or I care if an actress gets married or divorced, has a baby out of wedlock or goes into drug rehab? When a T.V. baseball announcer talks about someone's hundred million dollar seven-year contract, no one ever asks, "What's wrong with this picture?" I don't think that it's necessarily wrong for some billionaire to pay a skilled ballplayer big bucks. The problem, however, is that our political and economic structure completely rejects the talents and abilities of many of our "ordinary" citizens.

Sadly, there is little incentive for our political leaders to change anything, in spite of the rhetoric they spout while running for election. Their loyalties are firmly bound to the 1%; the wealthy citizens who are willing to finance their campaigns, and who enable our elected officials to become rich while in office and after they retire.

I believe that it is long past the point where Americans should be content to live vicariously through our athletes and entertainers. In this book, I will present a platform for meaningful change. **I will suggest concrete programs to repatriate jobs, reform the political system, and put an end to corruption in the banking and financial sectors. I will also recommend the implementation of a viable and cost-effective health care program to replace *Obamacare*. I will propose changes to our educational system and recommend specific reforms directed at our taxation system.**

You may not agree with each and every one of my proposals, but if you end up understanding and agreeing with the *concept* of Enlightened Capitalism, you will then be better equipped to use your most powerful weapon-your inalienable right to VOTE for change!

Question 2: **Do you agree that <u>Unbridled</u> Capitalism must be stopped before our society collapses and that the self-interests of our nation's Capitalists, present and future, must be tempered with *social responsibility*?**

Yes___ No___ Undecided___

Question 3: **Do you understand that advocating Enlightened Capitalism is in no way the same as embracing Communism?**

Yes___ No___ Undecided___

Chapter 2
Throw Them All Out
A Blueprint for Political Reform

I would like to refer you to an excellent book written by Peter Schweizer, which was published in 2011, entitled *"Throw Them All Out"*. This book is subtitled *"How politicians and their friends get rich off insider stock tips, land deals and cronyism that would send the rest of us to prison."* In his book, Mr. Schweizer provides details of specific schemes that have enabled politicians, from Presidents on down the line to the most junior congresspersons, to use their positions of power to attain wealth. Mr. Schweizer made a number of suggestions for political reform with which I agree but, so far, nothing has been done.

It's been a while since I read this book and I consciously have refrained from referring to it because I prefer to provide my own independent thoughts and ideas. No doubt, there will be some overlap. I will forward a copy of this book to Mr. Schweizer, but I want to make it clear that I have neither asked for nor received any feedback (either positive or negative) from him. If after reading this book, you endorse the concept of a grass roots movement advocating political and economic reform, I recommend

27

that you read Mr. Schweizer's book. It will give you additional motivation to seek change.

Let's begin with some basics. If I were to ask you, "Why do we have elected government officials?" you would probably respond, "That's a stupid question. Don't you know that it's totally impractical for (approximately) 240 million adults to weigh in on every single issue, major or minor?"

Believe it or not, I strongly suggest that's the wrong answer! As of April 2012, according to Pew Internet Reports, **only one in five American adults does not use the Internet. Technology opens up a whole new realm of opportunities for mass participation in decision making**.

Part of accepting change means recognizing that, what was the norm in the past, doesn't necessarily apply today, or as we move into the future. In the early 1900s, there was resistance to the adoption of the automobile. Today, life without cars is practically unthinkable. Around 1985, a good friend of mine who was a partner in one of the Big Four accounting firms, swore he'd never have a computer on his desk. (Yes, he has one today!)

Mr. Schweizer's book proves that the political system is broken. The whole process has degenerated into party politics, horse-trading for votes, knee-jerk responses to the lobbying efforts of special interest groups, and outright corruption. Today, *there is no reason why all ordinary Americans can't be polled on major matters and why our elected officials cannot be required to vote in accordance with the wishes of their constituents.*

I am <u>not</u> affiliated with either of the two major political parties in the United States. I am also not a member of any political organization whatsoever. I'd like to think, therefore, that the comments that follow are unbiased.

In order to explain why I believe that the political system has become broken, I'd like to go all the way back to the ratification of the U.S. Constitution and the unanimous acclamation of George Washington as our first President in 1788.

In my opinion, George Washington was really King George I of the United States, since the U.S. congressional system was actually modeled after the governing system in England. However, long before the U.S. Declaration of Independence was signed, the English King had become not much more than a figurehead. In the centuries following the ratification of the Magna Carta in 1215, an elected Parliament assumed the rights and responsibilities of English government. The last time a British monarch exercised the right to veto a measure passed by Parliament was in 1708. Today, the monarchy is simply part of a long ceremonial tradition that serves to unify the United Kingdom, although, to their credit, members of the royal family are involved in charitable and humanitarian endeavors.

In America, in contrast to the English "model", the Founding Fathers decided to invest its President with numerous powers, including the role of Commander-in-Chief of the armed forces, primary responsibility for the management of national and international affairs and the right to veto bills approved by Congress. Some of these powers were contained in the Constitution and some evolved over time. Harry S. Truman summed it up nicely with the sign on his desk that read "The Buck Stops Here."

Consider the many changes that have occurred over the past 250 years. In the early history of our nation, there was generally little need to consider anything more pressing than domestic issues- the concept of Manifest Destiny, which stood for America's quest to expand its borders from coast to coast. Compared to today, international trade was quite limited; there was no highly sophisticated stock market, and the U.S. did not have to deal with enemies armed with weapons of mass destruction.

In our times, it is clearly impossible for any one person to be knowledgeable and expert in all matters, both foreign and domestic. A President must therefore choose his or her advisors wisely. *If the only readily available advisors are motivated by political leanings or, even worse, accumulating personal wealth, I believe that it becomes relatively easy to mislead a President, even if his or her intentions are well-meaning.* In my opinion, possibly the best example of bad policy that may soon affect all of us is the adoption of "Obamacare".

Ask yourself why did George W. Bush invade Iraq? Was it the Iraqis who perpetrated 9/11? Did Saddam Hussein really harbor weapons of mass destruction? Was Mr. Bush largely motivated to "atone" for his father's decision not to send American troops into Baghdad in 1991? Or was his decision made, at least in part, to protect our sources of Middle East oil? What influence did Vice President Dick Cheney, whose company Halliburton was eventually awarded a total of $39.5 Billion in Iraq-related contracts, exert?

My point is <u>not</u> that the office of the President of the United States should be replaced. *We could, however, consider changing the method of how a President is chosen and, at the very least, do whatever we can to ensure that all Presidents receive sincere and unbiased advice.*

Perhaps the most important question we should ask is, what motivates people to vote for a particular Presidential candidate? Is it the party which he or she leads, or is it the person? If it is the party, then perhaps there should be no election. *The President might then simply become the leader of the party with the majority of seats in the House of Representatives. (Remember, I told you that many of my suggestions represent "out of the box thinking". Yes, some of my recommendations will be in violation of the U.S. Constitution as it now stands. However, please consider that decisions made in the 1780s are not necessarily the right ones for the 21st century.)*

Now, I would like to consider the evolution (or devolution) of Congress. Have you noticed that in the novels and movies of today, most elected officials are depicted as evil and/or corrupt? They are obsessed with their own agendas and even resort to violence and murder. Rogue Presidents and vice-Presidents are a favorite fiction topic as well.

Earlier, I referred to George Washington as America's King George, but without divine powers. **The U.S. Senate and House of Representatives were also modeled after the British system that consists of a House of Lords and a House of Commons. The main difference is that, in England, the House of Lords is *honorary* and rarely**

assumes an active role in creating or passing legislation.
Our neighbor to the north, Canada, has a Senate that
mirrors the British House of Lords in that members are
appointed and not elected. In England, membership in the
House of Lords is inherited. In Canada, appointment to the
Senate is generally in recognition of meritorious service to
the country. **In both cases, the "real" governing body
is the House of Commons, whose members are voted
in by their constituencies. They represent the various
political parties, each with its own platform.**

Neither Britain nor Canada has a President. Instead,
each political party elects a leader. **The leader of the party
with the most seats in the House of Commons becomes
the Prime Minister. In turn, the Prime Minister
appoints his or her cabinet members, generally from
persons who have also been elected to the Commons.** *At
any time, a party's "caucus" of senior members can vote
to replace the Prime Minister.*

Elections in Canada and The United Kingdom take
place every four years or so. **As long as one party holds a
majority of the seats, it can pass legislation unimpeded.**
The opposition parties can raise objections and these are
made known to the general public through the media. If
the public at large is displeased with the actions of the
governing party, it can vote an opposition party into power
in the next election. On occasion, a shift in power can
result in the reversal or amendment of prior legislation.

Both Britain and Canada have more than two well-
established parties. In cases where one party does not
garner a majority of the seats, two or more parties will
usually form a *coalition* and govern together. If and when

they can no longer agree, an election is called.

The "Parliamentary" system works well because those in power can govern without worrying about party politics. There is little need for "horse-trading" to get votes. As I just explained, if the general public becomes dissatisfied, there is always another election looming within the foreseeable future. In 1993, in an unprecedented situation, the governing Conservative Party that had held 169 seats in Canada's Parliament lost 167 of them!

In the United States, a very serious problem often occurs in cases where the President's political party does not control either or both divisions of Congress. The problem is magnified if different parties control the two houses. Legislation becomes watered-down and vote getting becomes a function of so-called horse-trading. The Federal government shutdown in October 2013 is a good example of party politics trumping matters of national importance.

I really enjoyed the movie *Lincoln* (**not** the movie Abe Lincoln- Vampire Hunter). *Lincoln* depicts the extent of the convoluted deal making and out-and-out blackmail that Abraham Lincoln had to resort to in order to push through the 13th Amendment to the Constitution in 1865 that abolished slavery. **And Mr. Lincoln did not have to contend with the 12,000 lobbyists that haunt our nation's capital today.**

Above, I suggested that the decision in 1787 to divide the U.S. Congress into two chambers was influenced, at least in part, by the system that was already a fixture of the governing system of England. *The Founding Fathers decided that two chambers would provide checks and balances, to forestall tyranny and carefully weigh both long-term and short-term implications of pending legislation.*

The House of Representatives was formulated to champion the *will of the people*. Memberships were, and still are, allocated based on relative population by state. California, at one extreme, has 53 representatives, while seven states only have one each. There are 435 seats in total. *The House has several exclusive powers, including the ability to initiate revenue bills, to impeach officials and* **to elect the U.S. President if there is no majority in the Electoral College.** *Members serve two-year terms.*

The existence of the Senate has, as its basis, the consensus of the Founding Fathers that each sovereign (self-governing) State should be **equally represented by two delegates**. *The exclusive powers of the Senate include ratifying treaties with other countries, and confirming the appointment of cabinet secretaries, federal judges and ambassadors. Members serve staggered six-year terms.*

In one sentence, the Founding Fathers envisioned the House as representing the will of the people and the Senate as being responsible for the nation as a whole. It is interesting that, while George Washington was a proponent of a bi-cameral framework for its ability to provide checks and balances, Thomas Jefferson advocated the efficiency of a single chamber only.

Enlightened Capitalism is only possible if our government can be made adhere to the concept of social responsibility, which necessitates representing all the people and not just the wealthy elite. The world has become far more complex than it was in 1787. We have made tremendous strides in our ability to expand, not only within our own borders, but our influences are also felt world-wide **Yet party politics, graft, corruption, and special–interest lobbying continue to hobble our society.** As we all know, lawmaking today is a time-consuming process and is, in many instances, watered down by political compromise

I therefore make the following recommendations:

1. All elections to both the House and the Senate should take place at *four-year intervals* as is the case *now* with Presidential elections.

I strongly believe that the current term of members of the House is too short. The system is costly and members must devote a disproportionate amount time worrying about re-election instead of concentrating on their legislative responsibilities. Further, since one must make hay while the sun shines, as the saying goes, there is the inclination to grab as much as possible for oneself in the short time allotted.

Four-year terms for Senators would serve to streamline the system. The current system of six-year staggered terms theoretically allows the senior Senator to teach the junior Senator from his or her State. However, *I believe that Senators should run on one ticket as a team since the function of the Senate should not be to champion any particular state but the **country as a whole**.*

2. The respective roles of the House of Representatives and the Senate should be redefined to eliminate overlap.

I suggest that each of the chambers should retain the exclusive powers they now enjoy. *Also, the House should be made specifically responsible for domestic issues, while the Senate's activities should be restricted primarily to matters affecting international relations.*

3. I recommend that Presidential elections should be abolished.

(This is probably the most revolutionary of all my proposals in this book.)

I believe that each party should elect a leader and a deputy leader *internally* who would become President and Vice-President respectively *if their party wins the majority of the seats in the House of Representatives.*

Each candidate for the presidency would campaign as they do now, emphasizing their own attributes and the major platforms of their respective parties.

As it already stands, it is not the popular vote that determines a winner. Rather it falls upon the Electoral College, whose membership is determined with reference to each state's relative population, to elect a President. Depending on its population, each state is allowed to appoint a certain number of representatives to the Electoral College. The members generally cast their ballots state-by-state in favor of the candidate who has received the most popular votes in that particular state. In Maine and Nebraska, the Electoral College votes may be split in proportion to the popular votes received by each candidate within the different districts. If my suggestion to choose the person who is the leader of the party that has the most seats in the House of Representatives as President is adopted, *the Electoral College would become redundant.*

Under my proposed system, the President would always be working in tandem with the House. It is true that the majority in the Senate could be comprised of members of the other (or another) party and the President would have to work with them on international matters. As is the case today, the President would retain the opportunity to address the Senate with his or her concerns and the right of a President to veto Senate bills would be retained.

4. Lobbying by special interest groups must be closely regulated.

In a free market system, including a framework based on Enlightened Capitalism, freedom of speech must be cherished. I am not suggesting that any particular industry or organization should be prohibited from hiring trained people to promote its interests. In fact, without advocates, our society might never change for the better. Without lobbyists, slavery might never have been abolished and women might never have obtained the right to vote. **There is nothing wrong if a special interest group decides to support one candidate over another. After all, each party would have its own platform.**

However, *I believe that lobbyists must be prevented by law from offering monetary or other personal incentives directly or indirectly to candidates for political office or members of their families.* **Restrictions should include paid vacations, the use of private jets, significant campaign financing and offers of employment and/or directorships.**

5. Campaign financing legislation must be regulated to impose reasonable limits.

I really don't have the necessary knowledge or experience to propose specific monetary limits, so I will restrict my comments to the concept of tightening the rules governing campaign financing only.

In 1976, the U.S. Supreme Court ruled that it would violate the First Amendment to limit what candidates could spend on their own behalf. In so ruling, the Supreme Court extended the right of free speech, perhaps beyond the original intentions of the people who drafted and approved this amendment.

Personally I believe that, since the First Amendment does not protect racism or hard-core pornography, the doctrine of unlimited campaign spending should not be protected either. *Let's amend the First amendment!*

Can one seriously expect someone who is a multi-millionaire or is a member of a multi-millionaire family to consistently represent the needs and wishes of the common people? John F. Kennedy once remarked during the 1960 West Virginia primary that he had received a telegram from his father telling him not to buy another vote since his father refused to pay for a landslide.

I believe that good government at the Federal level would be well served by requiring all (or at least virtually all) allowable campaign contributions to be made to the *national parties and not to candidates.* The parties themselves could then decide how much to allot to each candidate. A larger slice of the "pie" could be allocated to the people who are their parties' respective nominees for President and Vice President.

6. Let's regulate campaign spending

In this the 21st century, is it really necessary to clutter our environment with signs and placards that promote candidates for office? Is it not true that we can learn all we want to know from radio, T.V. and the Internet? Don't the various high-profile candidates debate each other? Aren't these debates recorded and posted on Youtube or Facebook? If you'd rather tune into hockey, basketball or a sit-com, can't you record candidate debates and watch them at some other time? Don't the candidates post bios and outlines of their platforms in the newspapers and in the voting pamphlets you receive prior to each election?

Again, I don't believe I can suggest monetary limits. **However, if campaign spending and campaign financing can be realistically curtailed, this would go a long way to reduce political dependency on special interest groups.**

7. The lawmakers must obey the law

I would now like to return to the first paragraph in this chapter where I referred to Peter Schweizer's expose of rampant political corruption. If the members of our Congress are the lawmakers of our nation in that they *create* our laws, we the people must, in turn, formulate effective methods to make sure they also obey them.

My first recommendation is to require each Congressperson and adult members of their immediate families to undergo annual audits to determine whether changes in their net worth are commensurate with reference to their legitimate incomes and personal net worth at the end of each preceding year. **These audits should continue until five years has elapsed after they have left office.** Penalties for corrupt activities should be as onerous as those in place under the provisions of RICO (Racketeer Influenced and Corrupt Organizations Act). These include criminal prosecution and confiscation of assets.

My second recommendation is to introduce the administration of periodic polygraph tests to members of Congress. Under current legislation, the Employee Polygraph Protection Act limits (but does not prohibit) employer use of lie detector tests. *However, Federal, State and local government employers are exempt from the Act.*

In general, a **public company employer** whose business is covered by the Act cannot require or even suggest that an employee or prospective employee take a polygraph test. The only exception is for investigations involving *economic loss or injury to the employer's business. This includes theft, embezzlement, misappropriation, or an act of unlawful industrial espionage or sabotage.*

These criteria could easily be adopted to test Congresspersons, especially when an audit turns up reasonable grounds for further investigation. The potential existence of offshore investments and/or corporations or trusts set up by others for the benefit of Congresspersons and their families should be a major focus of these tests.

8. Internet polls

Earlier, I mentioned that, historically, government representation was a necessity since one could never expect all citizens, or even only all *concerned* citizens, to weigh in on important matters with their opinions. This is actually no longer the case. The use of Internet polls now allows for mass participation. Granted, many existing polls are administered by organizations that have an agenda or bias. However, a government-sponsored **independent polling system** can be established through which our country's citizens can participate in referendums on "hot button" issues, such as gun control, illegal immigration, and same-sex marriages etc. I will discuss these and other contentious issues in a later chapter.

Identification of participants in these polls by way of social security numbers and birth dates would eliminate abuses that might otherwise arise from the casting multiple ballots. Participants' responses would be protected to eliminate privacy concerns. 21st Century technology can ensure that our government is one "Of the people, by the people and for the people".

Question 4: **Should all elections to the House of Representatives and the Senate be held at four-year intervals?**

Yes___ No___ Undecided___

Question 5: Should the leader of the party with the most seats in the House of Representatives automatically become President of the United States?

Yes___ No___ Undecided___

Question 6: Should the respective roles of the House of Representatives and the Senate be redefined to eliminate overlap?

Yes___ No___ Undecided___

Question 7: Should the House of Representatives be solely responsible for budgetary decisions and for domestic matters concerning the individual states?

Yes___ No___ Undecided___

Question 8: Should the Senate be solely responsible for matters affecting the security of the Nation as a whole including international relations?

Yes___ No___ Undecided___

Question 9: **Should lobbying by special interest groups be closely regulated to make it illegal to offer rewards in exchange for votes?**

Yes___ No___ Undecided___

Question 10: **Should campaign-financing rules be established that require National Parties, and not the Federal candidates themselves, to decide how funds are deployed?**

Yes___ No___ Undecided___

Question 11: **Should campaign spending be restricted?**

Yes___ No___ Undecided___

Question 12: **Do you support the concept of annual audits of the financial affairs of Members of Congress and their immediate families designed to expose irregularities?**

Yes___ No___ Undecided___

Question 13: **Do you support the concept of the annual audits suggested in Question 12 being extended until five years have elapsed after a Congressperson leaves office?**

Yes___ No___ Undecided

Question 14: **Do you support the administration of polygraph (lie detector) tests designed to detect bribes to Congresspersons and illegal acts?**

Yes___ No___ Undecided___

Question 15: **Do you support independent nation-wide referendums on contentious issues designed to obtain a consensus of public opinion?**

Yes___ No___ Undecided___

CHAPTER 3
JOBS, JOBS, JOBS

Social responsibility is a two-way street. The captains of industry must be convinced that they can gain significant advantages by tempering their greed in order to repatriate and create jobs. Then, if a substantial number of people are added to the labor force, workers' taxes coupled with a reduced need for government handouts, would allow for a *reduction in tax rates on the wealthy* as a reward for their initiatives.

Within an economic and political system that embraces Enlightened Capitalism, **management and labor can enjoy a symbiotic relationship, working together for the common good.**

Although you may initially find this concept really difficult to grasp, in a perfect system, *collective bargaining through labor unions becomes unnecessary.*

Here are the August 2013 unemployment statistics as provided by the Department of Labor.

Official unemployment percentage: 7.6%

Official number of unemployed people: **11.8 Million***

<u>Additional</u> number of potential workers who are no longer looking for work:	**2.6**	**Million**
Involuntary part-time employed people:	**8.2**	**Million**
Teenage unemployment percentage:		2 4 %
Veterans of Gulf Wars unemployment percentage:		9 . 9 %
African-American unemployment percentage:		13.7%
Hispanic unemployment percentage:		9 . 1 %

*There are 4.3 million people who have been unemployed for six months or longer.

There are 22.6 million people (the total of the numbers bolded above) who are unemployed or under-employed. **This is the approximate total of the *entire* populations of the eight most heavily populated cities in the United States**. (New York City, Los Angeles, Chicago, Houston, Philadelphia, Phoenix, San Antonio and San Diego.)

Of course, I don't believe anyone could ever expect 100% of all potential workers to have jobs. Perhaps full-employment might be attained in a totalitarian society where the government would have you shot if you refused to work. But this is certainly not a viable alternative for us in America!

To bring unemployment down to an acceptable rate of, say, below 4% involves taking a multi-faceted approach.

1. We must first focus on repatriating jobs that large corporations have shifted to third-world countries.

I have no quarrel with any U.S.-based enterprise that wants to expand into other countries *to service those foreign markets*. However, I take issue with American businesses that **lay-off American workers**, set up foreign subsidiaries, move their plants overseas, manufacture products through these subsidiaries and then export their products into the U.S. for sale to U.S. consumers. Most of the profit from the manufacturing process is not repatriated back into the U.S.

A loophole in the current tax system prevents U.S. taxes from being imposed as long as these foreign profits are left offshore. The current amount of such untaxed profits is estimated at **1.7 TRILLION dollars**. Lawmakers are currently debating whether or not to tax these profits and, if so at what rate. Some argue that there is no guarantee that taxing this money will actually help kick-start the American economy. The biggest companies could simply use the after-tax dollars to buy smaller companies without hiring more people.

I suggest that there is a viable compromise. **The solution is to calculate a *potential* tax payable on unrepatriated foreign profits at today's corporate tax rate of 35%, payable in ten equal annual installments. At the same time, an offsetting dollar-for-dollar 35% tax credit would be applied against money spent *out of repatriated funds* on the acquisition or construction of plants and equipment in the U.S. during this ten-year period, as well as on wages and benefits paid to new employees. (Any employees who are laid-off, leave or retire would offset the calculation of the number of new employees.)**

A simple example depicting some assumptions for one hypothetical company might help explain this concept:

Total amount of untaxed offshore profits:
$10,000,000

Potential tax payable (35%):
$3,500,000

Total tax potentially payable in **year 1** (one-tenth):
$350,000

Less: Invested in new equipment in **year 1:**
$286,000*x   35%   ($100,000)

Salaries/ benefits for 10 new employees **year 1**
$514,000*   x   35%:   ($180,000)

Tax payable: $70,000

*In this example to avoid the 35% tax entirely, the business would have had to repatriate and spend $1 million in year one (10% of $10 million). They actually spent $286,000+$514,000= $800,000. The business must therefore pay a tax of 35%x $200,000, or $70,000.

There are those who will argue that implementing my proposal would make it too expensive for U.S. consumers to buy goods made in the U.S.A, relative to goods imported from other countries. However, if domestic unemployment were substantially reduced and businesses began to once again invest in plants, equipment and inventories situated in the U.S., we would all be able to afford some increased costs in consumer goods.

For example, suppose you own a grocery store in a small American town. If five unemployed people who live within a 500-yard radius of your store find well-paying jobs and begin to shop at your store, your increased profit will likely more than counterbalance the additional cost of buying a few American-made T-shirts.

Basically, what I am advocating is a return to **Reaganomics as it was originally intended to operate in the early 1980s-management and employees working together to build a stronger America.**

2. My second recommendation is that our government and private industry make a concerted effort to advocate and sponsor an ongoing campaign to convince consumers to buy products made in *North America*.

In 1993, the United States, Canada and Mexico signed the North American Free Trade Association agreement (NAFTA). No doubt, the geographic proximity of the three countries precipitated this economic union, in the same way as the European Union (EU) was based on geographic considerations and was formed around the same time.

Conceptually, it makes sense to remove trade barriers between contiguous nations, but *an economic union only works well if there is a common business outlook and shared work ethic.* **In my opinion, Mexico on the one hand and the United States and Canada on the other have as little in common as Greece and Germany.** As we have seen, international trade agreements have done little to help the citizens of Mexico and Greece.

Perhaps former President Clinton believed that, by raising the Mexican standard of living, the flood of illegal immigration into the U.S would subside. Perhaps he believed that NAFTA would create an economic equilibrium. Even if this were the case, **building a framework of economic parity is a task that can take centuries, and not just a decade or two.**

Climate plays an important role in determining how cultures and civilizations evolve. The great British historian, Arnold Toynbee, postulated a concept called "challenge and response" in his ten-volume *"A Study of History"*. He said that, if a society responds efficiently to challenge, their civilization would grow while an inefficient response leads to stagnation. In part, Toynbee advanced the theory that climactic conditions great affect the ability to grow a civilization. If it is too cold, mankind must spend an inordinate amount of time just trying to survive and there is little opportunity to develop a complex civilization. If it is too hot, people become lethargic, especially if all they have to do is reach up and grab fruit from a tree to survive. Lethargy does not foster innovation.

In North America and Europe, inclement weather has certainly posed challenges over the centuries, but unfavorable conditions were never too extreme for sustained and uninterrupted periods of time. Climate challenges were met with progressive innovation as Western civilizations grew.

It is my belief that Canada and the U.S. share a great deal in common, even though Mexico, the third partner in NAFTA, does not share these commonalities. Canadians have learned a great deal from the U.S. because of exposure to American media- T.V., movies, books, periodicals etc. However, the reverse is not necessarily the case. As I will explain in this book, there are a number of things that Americans can learn from Canada, as well.

Here are a few facts worth mentioning about Canada beyond *traditional* language, social, and ethnic similarities to the U.S. First, with the exception of Edmonton, which grew as a result of some major oil discoveries in 1948, every other significant Canadian city is situated less than 150 miles from the U.S. border. If Toronto were located a few miles south of its actual location, it would be the fourth largest city by population in the U.S. Outside of the Province of Quebec, you will rarely hear French spoken and few Canadians commute to work by dog sled.

Canada is a resource-based economy while the United States is far more advanced in manufacturing. According to the U.S. Energy Information Administration, **The United States imports more petroleum products from Canada than from Saudi Arabia and Mexico *combined* with over half of imports from Venezuela thrown in for good measure!** *This fact is not well known by most Americans.*

In the 1980s, I developed and marketed what became Canada's best-selling income tax software. I insisted on buying my discs from the only Canadian supplier I could find and on having my manuals printed in Canada. Each of my software packages bore a "Made in Canada" label. I could have purchased these materials cheaper outside the country, but I could see, even back then, that domestic jobs were falling by the wayside and, in my own small way, I decided not to succumb to greed. I was making more than

51

enough money at the time so there really wasn't much of a sacrifice required.

Sometime in the late 1980s, I was at a conference and I heard the first woman to become a partner in the Canadian arm of the multi-national accounting firm PricewaterhouseCoopers speak about a junket she had taken to China. The participants on that trip were taken to inspect an automobile plant and someone exclaimed, "So, that's where it went!" It seems that General Motors had completely dismantled one of its North American plants and had reassembled it piece by piece in China.

I believe we should all make a conscious effort to buy vehicles that contain parts manufactured and assembled mainly in North America. We should encourage North American clothing manufacturers to prominently display labels proclaiming that their products are made in the U.S.A. or Canada, and we should try to purchase furniture and accessories that are made in North America.

Remember, if we all do our part to bolster the overall economy, our collective ability to earn more will easily offset the additional costs we would incur by buying domestically produced goods. Capitalism with a conscience will still support the North American entrepreneurial and innovative spirit.

3. We must make rules to regulate executive remuneration.

The best argument to support the regulation of executive remuneration can be presented by examining a few numbers:

Ratio of average U.S. Chief Executive Officer (CEO) pay to average worker pay:

1980: 44 to 1

1990: 107 to 1

2012: 283 to 1

According to a recent MSN Money article by Michael Brush, the largest U.S. companies paid their Chief Executive Officers (CEOs) an average of **$5000** an hour in 2012. **These CEOs earned more in *11 hours* than the typical family earned in a year.**

Much of the remuneration of senior executives of public companies is derived from stock options. They receive the right to buy shares of their employer company at the current price and they may exercise that right at some future time. If the stock drops in value, they decline the option and walk away with no loss. If the stock rises, they exercise their rights and, if they sell immediately, earn a before-tax profit equal to the rise in the share price since the option was granted. (If they keep the shares the tax bite may be reduced if certain capital gains allowances come into play.)

From personal experience, I can assure you that, today, no one really "needs" an after-tax income of more than $1 Million a year to live *comfortably*. You may not be able to buy a new Bentley every year and you may be "forced" to live in a home with a living area of "only" 3,500 sq. ft. You may also have to cut back a bit on your travel and you might have to fly economy once in a while. Sorry-no private jet! However, you will easily be able to send a couple of kids to private schools. You will probably own two late model cars (hopefully made in North America) and a cabin retreat. You won't have to skimp on food.

Of course, senior executives do thrive on incentives and a framework of Enlightened Capitalism must continue to provide reasonable incentives. Below are the measures I propose:

I believe that the maximum annual remuneration paid to any individual executive (whether by salary, benefits, stock options, or any other means of compensation) should *initially* be set at a level of $1.5 Million dollars. I also believe that the maximum tax rate on earned income of up to $1.5 Million should be set at 33.3%* and that these rules should apply to all U.S. companies, public and private, with five or more employees.

Once this level of remuneration is reached, I propose that additional compensation could then be paid <u>provided </u>*each employee who has been with that employer for at least two years receives a bonus of at least 5% of the average additional remuneration in excess of $1.5 Million paid out to all the executives who receive more than this base amount.* The 5% bonuses would then comprise part of each employee's base pay for the subsequent and succeeding years.

In the event that any executive's income in a given year exceeds $1.5 million because of stock option

benefits that could not be estimated or quantified in advance and the required bonuses to the other employees are not paid, the executive would be required to *refund the excess compensation* to the company.

I also recommend that retirement payments and "golden parachute" payments to executives whose employment has been terminated because of a buy-out should be limited a reasonable formula based on up to three times average remuneration for the previous three years.

For purposes of these rules, if a group of related companies exists, all remuneration paid to any one person would have to be added together to avoid circumventing the income limits. Companies and their executives will be prohibited from avoiding these rules through the payment of consulting fees.

*Please note that I have indirectly introduced a proposal recommending that the maximum tax rate on earned income be set at 33.3%. I don't believe that it is really beneficial to impose higher taxes on the non-investment-related earnings of those relatively few people who "drive" our economy. I believe that the solution to a substantial portion of the U.S. deficit problem can be found by increasing the tax base and not the tax rate.

As I've said earlier, for the principles of Enlightened Capitalism to be effective, a greater number of people must *become payers of taxes,* with a corresponding reduction in the numbers who are dependent on government handouts. Again, *social responsibility is a two way street!*

And now, for another blockbuster:

4. If a workable system can be put in place so that senior executives start sharing the wealth more fairly with their employees, is there really a need for unions in the private sector?

Historically, the main role of unions has been collective bargaining. If a profit-sharing system such as the one I just described is implemented, this function falls off the table. Government already sets a minimum wage. OSHA (Occupational Safety and Health Administration) deals with situations involving safety and health. The only other major potential issue is specific employee grievances. These can be handled either by internally established management-labor committees or by way of mediation if the particular business is small. Please note, *I believe that unions should retain their roles to support teachers, government employees and others employed in the public sector.*

5. An analysis of tax rates

Financialsamuri.com prepared the table below in April 2011:

Based on the Internal Revenue Service's 2010 database, here's how much the top Americans made:

Top 1%: $380,354

Top 5%: $159,619

Top 10%: $113,799

Top 25%: $67,280

Top 50%: > $33,048

SUMMARY OF FEDERAL INDIVIDUAL INCOME TAX DATA, 2010

	Number of Returns w/ Positive AGI	AGI ($ millions)	Income Taxes Paid ($ millions)	Group's Share of Total AGI	Group's Share of Income Taxes	Income Split Point	Average Tax Rate (Effective)
All Taxpayers	139,960,580	8,426,625	1,031,512	100%	100%		12.24%
Top 1%	1,399,606	1,685,472	392,149	20%	38%	$380,354	23.27%
Top 5%	6,998,029	2,926,701	605,718	34.73%	58.72%	$159,619	20.70%
Top 10%	13,996,058	3,856,462	721,421	45.77%	69.94%	$113,799	18.71%
Top 25%	34,990,145	5,678,179	890,614	67.38%	86.34%	$67,280	15.68%
Top 50%	69,980,290	7,352,111	1,003,639	87.25%	97.30%	>$33,048	13.65%
Bottom 50%	69,980,290	1,074,514	27,873	12.75%	2.70%	<$33,048	2.59%

Source: IRS 2010

Only the top 1% of all Americans earned over $380,000 in 2010. Yet they paid 38% of all personal taxes. That is why I don't believe it is necessary to tax earned income at any rate higher than 33.3%. *The only "benefit" that the imposition of higher taxes on the wealthy provides, is to make the rest of the population less resentful.* On the other hand, higher rates encourage the wealthy to use all means possible to avoid or reduce their burden.

The top 50% of taxpayers earns in excess of $33,000 a year and *this top 50% pays over 97% of the total tax bite.*

6. The bottom 50% pays virtually no tax at all.

The Tax Policy Center, based in Washington D.C., provides an independent analysis of tax issues and communicates their findings to policymakers and the public. According to this group's analysis, the bottom 50% falls into three main groups:

The elderly

The working poor who pay no taxes as a result of the

earned income credit and child tax credits

Low- income families who, by claiming the standard deduction and personal exemptions, pay no tax on up to around $27,000 to $30,000, depending on the number of persons in the household.

From these statistics, it becomes obvious that shifting income from wealthy "employers" to their employees is not enough to create a vibrant economy. Bringing back jobs from foreign countries is potentially a big step in the right direction, but this too is not enough. **What is also needed is a concerted effort at job creation.**

7. Meaningful job creation

At the beginning of this chapter, I provided some unemployment statistics. I repeat a few of them here to create a focus.

Teenage unemployment percentage: 24%

Veterans of Gulf Wars unemployment percentage: 9.9%

African-American unemployment percentage: 13.7%

Hispanic unemployment percentage: 9.1%

It is no secret that, like many of his predecessors, President Obama's administration is concerned about unemployment. Borrowing a page from former President Franklin D. Roosevelt, Mr. Obama has suggested that the Federal government should concentrate on job creation by improving and fixing *"infrastructure assets"*, such as roads, highways, shipyards etc. I agree that **there really is no other solution that can completely solve the puzzle.**

Step one is to repatriate lost jobs and give them

back to the skilled workers who lost them. **Step two is to educate our young people and offer them something other than low-paying jobs in the hospitality industry**.

The Republican Party has traditionally opposed additional government spending. However, it only makes sense to me that, if people are given jobs that provide them with adequate disposable incomes, they will spend their earnings, in turn creating more jobs and more government revenues.

In a Capitalist system, especially one that is tempered by the concept of social responsibility, I believe that the private sector should take on the task for supervising actual infrastructure development and re-development. Private industry has the experience and the management expertise. Employees provided by the federal government, at least in the initial stages, can well furnish the (initially) unskilled manual labor.

I suggest that the responsibility for hiring and training should be given to America's military and that, wherever possible Gulf War veterans should fill supervisory positions. Almost 10% of Gulf War veterans are currently unemployed. These people are used to military discipline and can be come excellent mentors for America's youth.

To accomplish this, I also suggest that the U.S. should institute a **peacetime draft** employing methods similar to the ones applied by President Roosevelt in the 1930s to alleviate unemployment during the Great Depression. I recommend that all young people, ages 18-24 should be required to participate for *a three-year period* **unless they qualify for an exemption.** Exemptions would be provided to anyone who;

-Is certified by medical practitioners to be either physically or mentally handicapped

-Can show evidence of regular gainful employment that is expected to continue

-Is a student pursuing a degree or diploma at a recognized educational facility.

If draftees are in relationships and/or have dependents, the government should ensure that they are based at work sites that limit the need for long-distance commutes.

Persons over the age of 24 should be permitted to "enlist" if they wish to do so and participants may voluntarily extend their "tours of duty".

An important component of this program should be the assurance that no person would be forced to engage in any *foreign* military activities or combat unless they volunteer.

I recommend that a five-day workweek should be allocated between three days of infrastructure-based assignments and two days of education, including (among other possibilities) remedial basic education, technology programs, and training as mechanics. An option should be offered to allow draftees to sign up for traditional military training on a part-time basis along the lines of programs already provided by the National Guard.

I believe that there should be no civil or criminal penalty for failure to participate. *However, anyone who*

is eligible to participate and declines should not receive any government handouts.

Pay scales should approximate the amounts paid by the military to persons not engaged in combat. If the current military pay scale assumes that lodging and food are provided, the pay of participants in the above program should be adjusted to cover reasonable costs that they themselves would incur in cases where they maintain their own residences.

Finally, I suggest that anyone older than age 24, who is not a senior or is not handicapped, should be required to provide infrastructure project support services, such as laundry, food preparation etc., each in accordance with their particular capabilities, *if their only other alternative is to be dependent on welfare or social assistance.* Most infrastructure projects would probably be large enough to provide daycare services for the young children of workers. Wherever possible, single parents who previously had to rely on social assistance should be trained to supervise these facilities.

8. Illegal immigration

My last topic in this chapter concerns illegal immigration. Yet again, I reiterate my opinion that charity begins at home. As I write this, there is a proposal under discussion to give amnesty to 12 Million illegal immigrants. This is **an issue that I believe should be decided by a nation-wide referendum and not by the President and/ or Congress.**

Personally, I find it difficult to support such an amnesty on the grounds that I believe we must first solve our country's unemployment problem and make sure our bona-fide citizens and residents earn a reasonable wage. I am certainly in favor of admitting people into the Unites States who, by virtue of their qualifications and skills, bring us expertise that we would not otherwise have. I also have compassion for people who must flee from racial or religious persecution. However, I draw the line at giving legal status to anyone who simply sees the United States as a meal ticket.

There are those among us, generally the more affluent, who welcome illegal immigrants as a source of cheap labor. Gardeners, housekeepers, nannies, fruit-pickers, manual laborers, etc. Obviously, if there were no illegal immigrants, employers would have to pay more for these services. **However, paying more would reduce domestic unemployment and provide many Americans with more money to spend.** Overall, I believe the U.S. economy would benefit from this "trickle down" effect.

If we as a nation decide to take action to eliminate illegal immigration, there are really only two steps that must be taken to solve the problem.

The first is to remove any and all opportunities for an illegal to work. Anyone who offers employment to someone, whether in a business or for personal purposes, must be given the right to examine an applicant's proof of legal status. An example of such proof would be a Green Card, a valid Social Security Card or a U.S. passport. If one is convicted of knowingly employing an illegal, a first offence should carry a minimum penalty of $10,000. The penalty needs to be sufficiently onerous to discourage second offenses.

The second step is to deny the admission of children of illegal immigrants into any U.S. school *even if these children were born here*. Such children would also be denied automatic U.S. citizenship. In order for a child to be granted U.S. citizenship, I suggest that our laws should be amended so that the child's birth mother is required to prove a valid status. Failure to do so would result in deportation of both mother and child. When a child enters school, the person who has legal custody should be required to prove his or her legal status in the U.S. before the child is admitted.

I really don't expect that the result of these rules will result in mass deportations. I believe most illegals would leave of their own accord if they cannot work or obtain rights to education.

Question 16: **Do you agree that untaxed foreign profits of American companies should be taxed at regular corporate tax rates, unless they are repatriated and used to acquire or construct plants and equipment in the U.S. and/or are used to pay wages and benefits to new employees?**

Yes___ No___ Undecided___

Question 17: **Do you agree that our government and private industry should sponsor an ongoing campaign to convince consumers to buy products made in North America?**

Yes___ No___ Undecided___

Question 18: Do you agree that basic executive remuneration should be capped by legislation and that additional compensation should be allowed <u>only</u> if <u>each</u> employee who has been with the company for at least two years receives a bonus of at least 5% of the average additional remuneration paid out to all executives who will earn in excess of the maximum base remuneration?

Yes___ No___ Undecided___

Question 19: **Should the basic executive remuneration of senior executives be capped at $1.5 Million (in today's dollars)?**

Yes___ No. It should be higher___ No. It should be lower___ Undecided___

Question 20: **Do you think executive retirement payments and termination ("Golden Parachute") payments resulting from buy-outs should be limited to three times average remuneration for the previous three years?**

Yes___ No___ Undecided___

Question 21: **Do you agree that the maximum Federal tax on earned income should not exceed 33.3% to provide reasonable incentives for innovation and leadership?**

Yes___ No___ Undecided____

Question 22: **Do you agree that, if management shared remuneration equitably with employees, there would be little need for unions in the private sector, except to handle employee grievances?**

Yes___ No___ Undecided___

Question 23: **Do you agree that steps should be taken to reduce unemployment by having the government fund infrastructure development and redevelopment, including roads, bridges and highways?**

Yes___ No___ Undecided___

Question 24: **Do you agree that the military should be given the task of hiring and training employees to work on infrastructure projects and that Gulf War veterans should be given preference to fill supervisory positions?**

Yes___ No___ Undecided___

Question 25: **Do you agree that the U.S. should institute a peacetime draft under which young people, who are not in school, already working or incapacitated, should be required to participate for a three-year period for the purpose of carrying out infrastructure development and redevelopment projects? (No person drafted under this proposal would be required to engage in any military activities or combat outside of American soil unless they volunteer.)**

Yes___ No___ Undecided___

Question 26: **Do you agree that the activities of inductees should be divided between infrastructure-based assignments and educational pursuits that are tailored to each individual's interests and aptitudes?**

Yes___ No___ Undecided___

Question 27: **Do you agree that anyone who is required to participate in the draft and refuses should be prohibited from receiving any government handouts?**

Yes___ No___ Undecided___

Question 28: **Do you agree that anyone who is not a senior or handicapped and is dependent on government handouts should be required to provide support services (e.g. food preparation, laundry etc.) to the infrastructure projects, each in accordance with their capabilities?**

Yes___ No___ Undecided___

Question 29: **Do you support President Obama's proposal to give 12 Million illegal immigrants amnesty and a path to citizenship?**

Yes___ No___ Undecided___

Question 30: **Do you agree that the issue of amnesty for illegal immigrants should be decided by a nation-wide referendum?**

Yes___ No___ Undecided___

Question 31: **Do you agree that illegals should not be allowed to work in the U.S.?**

Yes___ No___ Undecided___

Question 32: **Do you agree that anyone who knowingly employs an illegal should be heavily fined?**

Yes___ No___ Undecided___

Question 33: **Do you believe that children born in the U.S. to illegal immigrants should be denied U.S. citizenship?**

Yes___ No___ Undecided___

Question 34: **Do you believe that the children of illegal aliens should be denied admission to U.S schools?**

Yes___ No___ Undecided___

CHAPTER 4
REFORMING FINANCIAL MARKETS

Of the 442 Billionaires in the United States, Forbes.com lists 102 whose main source of wealth is "investments" and another 21 who became mega-wealthy through financing. This is just under 30% of the total. Many of these people have neither created new technologies nor developed new sources of energy. They did not manufacture anything and they did not supply us with food and beverages. They didn't even entertain us!

They are, of course, facilitators in that they arrange the funding for most of our country's larger enterprises. Judging from the statistics pertaining to billionaires, I would expect that a disproportionate percentage of the *multi-millionaires* also accumulated their wealth through investing and financing.

Investing in the stock market is often referred to as a "zero sum game". Money is neither created nor destroyed. For every dollar "won", someone else "loses" a dollar. The same concept applies to casinos, and, as is the case with casinos, the "house" usually wins.

In this case, the house is comprised of banks, insurance companies, hedge funds (to be defined), brokerage firms and commodity traders. **The deck is stacked against the small investor.**

If a framework of Enlightened Capitalism is to work effectively, measures must be implemented to level the playing field.

In this chapter, I will deal with financial markets, including commodities and derivatives (which are not as complicated as they first appear). I will offer suggestions for establishing rules that are fair to all Americans. I will also discuss the deficiencies of existing accepted accounting principles and practices and how these may be corrected.

We are all aware that we are living in an era in which interest rates are the lowest in well over half a century. With the collapse of housing prices and massive unemployment, our government has had no choice but to choose two simultaneous courses of action.

The first was to **print money.** Yes, they have done that, but printing too much money debases a country's currency and can lead to a monetary collapse. **According to cnsnews.com, the national debt has increased by $5.9 TRILLION dollars during Mr. Obama's Presidency, which is more than its increase under all Presidents from George Washington through Bill Clinton combined.** (Personally, I believe that most of the blame for this should be placed squarely on the shoulders of former President

George W. Bush and his administration.)

So far, the U.S. government has been able to get away with operating the printing presses non-stop because the U.S. dollar is the world's **reserve currency**. International debts are settled in U.S. dollars. Our dollar is also used to denominate commodity prices such as gold and oil. Other countries, notably China, are beginning to question whether international monetary policies should be amended to perhaps mandate several alternative reserve currencies. If the rules of the game are changed, there is every likelihood that the U.S. dollar would lose a great deal of its value.

The best analogy I can present is to ask you what would happen in the long-term if you could pay all your personal debts with Monopoly money. Every time you ran out, all you would have to do is go to the store and buy a new game. (I think you can actually buy packages of Monopoly money without even purchasing the entire game.) Sooner or later, your creditors will simply refuse to extend you any more credit.

Beyond printing money, the second course of action that was taken by our government over the last few years was to **drastically lower interest rates.** Lowering interest rates was intended to kick-start business as well as personal spending and permit people to refinance and keep their homes. To a large extent, this policy has worked reasonably well. It has permitted businesses to reduce their financing costs and has led to a gradual slow-down in the number of mortgage foreclosures. Arguably, the largest beneficiary of low interest rates has been the U.S. government itself. By lowering the interest rate on its *own debt*, our government has been able to keep its deficits from rising as quickly as they otherwise would have risen.

However, there have also been adverse consequences resulting from these policies. There are over 40 Million Americans who are age 65 or older. Historically, seniors have been risk-averse and were content to park their savings in secure interest-bearing investments. Since it is no longer possible to find such investment vehicles with decent yields, *millions of people have been forced into the giant casino that the stock market has become.* While some have prospered, it is a well-known fact that markets fluctuate. When they do drop, they tend to fall precipitously as investors panic.

In my next chapter, I will explain how low interest rates have had a disastrous effect on **pension plan performance** and show you that, even **if *you* do not invest *directly*, your post-retirement income is now at serious risk. I believe it is crucial for all of us to understand the basics of how financial markets operate and the impact of changeable interest rates.**

Currently, there is much Federal Reserve and media discussion about the advisability of "tapering off" from the low-rate stimulus program. Any time this possibility (probability?) is brought up, shock waves reverberate through our markets. Here's an analogy. If you offer candy to a baby on a daily basis and then suddenly withdraw these treats, you will have one confused and angry kid on your hands.

In order to present suggestions on how to "level the playing field", I think that it's necessary to explain why the playing field has become such a minefield for most Americans.

Historically, as businesses started up or grew, it became necessary for them to raise capital by enticing people to invest in exchange for ownership interests. Investors would therefore contribute money and receive shares in exchange. For example, if you bought one share out of a total of 100 shares issued, you would own 1% of a particular business.

Naturally, an investor could not realistically be expected to hold his or her investment forever, so it then became necessary to create a mechanism through which shares could be bought and sold.

A free market system was therefore initially established to permit buyers and sellers to transact at fair market values through a system involving bids to buy and offers to sell. If a buyer's offer was too low, he or she might have to raise it in order to acquire an investment, while, conversely, if there were more sellers than buyers, a seller might have to lower the asking price in order to sell.

Over the centuries, certain individuals and firms became very astute in evaluating investments and potential investments and, instead of transacting in order to participate in the long-term fortunes of particular companies, they became *short-term traders of securities*.

Technology has been of great benefit to most of us. However, I believe no one has profited more than well-capitalized professional traders and their firms. They now have access to powerful computers that can instantaneously analyze perhaps hundreds of variables that can affect a particular stock's short-term price movements. These variables include dissecting a company's reported financial data, comparisons to other companies in the same industry, commodity prices as they might affect a business's profitability, as well as peripheral factors, such as international economic and political conditions and major current events. There are also computer programs that analyze overall investor sentiment, government news releases (such as employment reports) and statements by the Federal Reserve, politicians, economists and business leaders. The list of variables is almost endless.

Now, I believe that *there is nothing wrong with using all available technological aids to make prudent investment decisions.* The genie is out of the bottle and the impact of technology is irreversible. Individual investors can take advantage of these technologies by working with investment houses and brokerage firms that have good track records and reputations.

There are already laws in place that require advisors to disclose whether they have made investments in the securities they are recommending. There are also strict laws in place to prevent the use of inside information- knowledge of significant events that have not as yet been disclosed to the public at large- for unfair advantage.

There are also provisions that require public companies to disclose such significant events within four business days and for insiders to report their own purchases or sales of a company's shares within two business days.

So why then is the playing field **NOT** level?

The answer is twofold: **short selling and day trading**.

If I wanted to, could I legally sell the Brooklyn Bridge to you? Of course not! Why? **Because I don't own it!**

If the law won't allow me to sell the Brooklyn Bridge, how can I sell you shares in a company that I don't own? Well, surprisingly, *I can, as long as I can "cover" my position at some time in the future.*

The legal right to short stocks and even whole markets to create investor panic gives wealthy people a very unfair advantage over everyone else. If I believe that a particular company's stock will *fall* within a short time, nothing stops me from shorting the stock and selling a couple of hundred shares, in the hope that I could buy them back at a lower price later on. I would simply have to *sit and wait* for events to unfold.

On the other side of the coin, if several fund managers and/or investment houses got together and shorted a few *million* shares, flooding the market would *automatically cause the price to drop*. Small investors would quickly panic thereby precipitating an even larger decline. At the right time, the "big boys" would cover their positions while the "little guys" would be wiped out.

When I did some research on the origin of short selling, I came across a fascinating article on Wikipedia. I think it makes for worthwhile reading.

"Some hold that the practice was invented in 1609 by Dutch merchant Isaac Le Maire, a sizeable shareholder of the Vereenigde Oostindische Compagnie (VOC). Short selling can exert downward pressure on the underlying stock, driving down the price of shares of that security. This, combined with the seemingly complex and hard to follow tactics of the practice, have made short selling a historical target for criticism. **At various times in history, governments have restricted or banned short selling.**

The London banking house of Neal, James, Fordyce and Down collapsed in June 1772, precipitating a major crisis which included the collapse of almost every private bank in Scotland, and a liquidity crisis in the two major banking centers of the world, London and Amsterdam. The bank had been speculating by shorting East India Company stock on a massive scale, and apparently using customer deposits to cover losses. It was perceived as having a magnifying effect in the violent downturn in the Dutch tulip market in the eighteenth century. In another well-referenced example, George Soros became notorious for "breaking the Bank of England" on Black Wednesday of 1992, when he sold short more than $10 billion worth of pounds sterling.

The term "short" was in use from at least the mid-nineteenth century. It is commonly understood that "short" is used because the short-seller is in a deficit position with his brokerage house. Jacob Little was known as The Great Bear of Wall Street who began shorting stocks in the United States in 1822.

Short sellers were blamed for the Wall Street Crash of 1929. Regulations governing short selling were implemented in the

United States in 1929 and in 1940. Political fallout from the 1929 crash led Congress to enact a law banning short sellers from selling shares during a downtick; this was known as the uptick rule, and this was in effect until July 3, 2007 when the Securities and Exchange Commission removed it. President Herbert Hoover condemned short sellers and even J. Edgar Hoover said he would investigate short sellers for their role in prolonging the Depression. A few years later, in 1949, Alfred Winslow Jones founded a fund (that was unregulated) **that bought stocks while selling other stocks short, hence hedging some of the market risk, and the hedge fund was born."**

(My Note: a hedge fund is simply an investment pool that can either go long or short based on the decisions of its management.)

"Negative news, such as litigation against a company, may also entice professional traders to sell a stock short in hope of the stock price going down.

During the Dot-com bubble, shorting a start-up company could backfire since it could be taken over at a price higher than the price at which speculators shorted. Short-sellers were forced to cover their positions at acquisition prices, while in many cases the firm often overpaid for the start-up.

Naked short selling restrictions

During the 2008 financial crisis, critics argued that investors taking large short positions in struggling financial firms like Lehman Brothers, HBOS and Morgan Stanley created instability in the stock market and placed additional downward pressure on prices. In response, a number of countries introduced restrictive regulations on short selling in 2008 and 2009. Investors argued that it was in the weakness of financial institutions, not short selling, that drove stocks to fall. In September 2008, the Securities Exchange Commission in the United States abruptly banned short sales, primarily in financial stocks, to protect companies under siege in the stock market. That ban expired several weeks later as regulators determined the ban was not stabilizing the price of stocks.

Temporary short-selling bans were also introduced in the United Kingdom, Germany, France, Italy and other European countries in 2008 to minimal effect. Australia moved to ban naked short selling entirely in September 2008. Germany placed a temporary ban on naked short selling of certain euro zone securities in 2010.Spain and Italy introduced short selling bans in 2011 and again in 2012. **Worldwide, economic regulators seem inclined to restrict short selling to decrease potential downward price cascades. Investors continue to argue this only contributes to market inefficiency.**

Short selling stock consists of the following:

- The speculator instructs the broker to sell the shares and the proceeds are credited to his broker's account at the firm upon which the firm can earn interest. Generally, the short seller does not earn interest on the short proceeds and cannot use or encumber the proceeds for another transaction.

- Upon completion of the sale, the speculator has 3 days (in the US) to borrow the shares. If required by law, the speculator first ensures that cash or equity is on deposit with his brokerage firm as collateral for the initial short margin requirement. Some short sellers, mainly firms and hedge funds, participate in the practice of naked short selling, where the shorted shares are not borrowed or delivered.

- The speculator may close the position by buying back the shares (called covering). If the price has dropped, he makes a profit. If the stock advanced, he takes a loss.

- Finally, the speculator may return the shares to the lender or stay short indefinitely.

- At any time, the lender may call for the return of his shares e.g. because he wants to sell them. The borrower must buy shares on the market and return them to the lender (or he must borrow the shares from elsewhere). When the broker completes this transaction automatically, it is called a 'buy-in'.

Shorting stock in the U.S.

In the U.S., in order to sell stocks short, the seller must arrange for a broker-dealer to confirm that it is able to make delivery of the shorted securities. This is referred to as a "locate." Brokers have a variety of means to borrow stocks in order to facilitate locates and make good delivery of the shorted security.

The vast majority of stocks borrowed by U.S. brokers come from loans made by the leading custody banks and fund management companies. Institutions often lend out their shares in order to earn a little extra money on their investments. The custodian who holds the securities for the institution usually arranges these institutional loans. In an institutional stock loan, the borrower puts up cash collateral, typically 102% of the value of the stock. The lender, who often rebates part of the interest to the borrower, then invests the cash collateral. The interest that is kept by the lender is the compensation to the lender for the stock loan.

Brokerage firms can also borrow stocks from the accounts of their own customers. Typical margin account agreements give brokerage firms the right to borrow customer shares without notifying the customer. In general, brokerage accounts are only allowed to lend shares from accounts for which customers have "debit balances", meaning they have borrowed from the account. An SEC Rule imposes such severe restrictions on the lending of shares from cash accounts or excess margin (fully paid for) shares from margin accounts that most brokerage firms do not bother except in rare circumstances. (These restrictions include that the broker must have the express permission of the customer and provide collateral or a letter of credit.)

Most brokers will allow retail customers to borrow shares to short a stock only if one of their own customers has purchased the stock on margin. Brokers will go through the "locate" process outside their own firm to obtain borrowed shares from other brokers only for their large institutional customers.

Stock exchanges such as the NYSE or the NASDAQ typically report the "short interest" of a stock, which gives the number of shares that have been *legally* sold short as a percent of the total float. Alternatively, these can also be expressed as the short interest ratio, which is the number of shares *legally* sold short as a multiple of the average daily volume. These can be useful tools to spot trends in stock price movements but in order to be reliable, investors must also ascertain the number of shares brought into existence by naked shorters. Speculators are cautioned to remember that for every share that has been shorted (owned by a new owner), a 'shadow owner' exists (i.e. the original owner) who also is part of the universe of owners of that stock, i.e. Despite not having any voting rights, he has not relinquished his interest and some rights in that stock."

My strong recommendation is that shorting of shares on any U.S. stock exchange should be completely *outlawed*. Taking this step would go a long way towards leveling the playing field for all Americans.

In recent years, new investment vehicles have emerged called Exchange-Traded Funds (ETFS). An ETF holds assets such as stocks, bonds, commodities and currencies and trades close to its net asset value during the trading day. There are also ETFs that track an index, such as the Standard & Poor 500 and the Dow Jones Industrial Average. An ETF is an example of a "derivative." *A derivative is simply an investment vehicle that is derived from something else, called the "underlying".* For example, the value of a Dow Jones Industrial Average Fund at any moment in time is *derived from the underlying values* of the stocks of thirty large U.S. corporations. No magic!

Really!

Conceptually, an ETF is an interesting concept since one can, for example, buy into an index fund, like a Dow Jones Industrial Average fund, instead of trying to buy into thirty different stocks. An ETF shares many characteristics of a mutual fund. **However, the downside is that *they can also be used by the very wealthy to manipulate markets, since there are also ETFs that are set up to <u>short</u> specific classes of investments.***

I therefore recommend that a prohibition on shorting be extended to U.S. ETFs as well.

The second impediment to a level playing field is the concept of **day trading**. Again, I quote from the good folks at Wikipedia:

"**Day trading** is speculation in securities, specifically buying and selling financial instruments within the same trading day, such that all positions are usually closed before the market close for the trading day. Traders who participate in day trading are called active traders or day traders. Traders, who trade in this capacity with the motive of profit, assume the capital markets role of speculator.

Some of the more commonly day-traded financial instruments are stocks, stock options, currencies, and a host of futures contracts such as equity index futures, interest rate futures, and commodity futures.

Day trading used to be an activity that was exclusive to financial firms and professional speculators. Many day traders are bank or investment firm employees working as specialists in equity investment and fund management. However, with the advent of electronic trading and margin trading, day trading has become increasingly popular among at-home traders."

Conceptually, since our society permits betting on horse racing, I believe that (*as long as shorting becomes prohibited*) day trading is acceptable. However, institutions have access to computer power that the average day trader lacks. There have been many allegations that these institutions can "jump ahead of the market" to get their orders filled before ordinary investors and that they sometimes get sensitive information several milliseconds ahead of everyone else. This allows them to use their computing power to place orders before news is released.

To level things out, I propose 10% surtax on net day trading profits of all <u>financial institutions</u> (both publicly and privately owned).

I would now like to examine the subject of **commodities trading**.

The term "commodities" covers a broad spectrum of goods, ranging from sugar, corn, soybeans and pork bellies right through precious metals such as gold, silver and platinum. Oil, coal and natural gas are other examples of commodities.

Commodities trading was initially a natural extension of normal business activities. A sugar producer might want to insure a guaranteed price for its crop. The business could therefore sell its *future production* by contract to one or more buyers. One of these buyers might be a chocolate bar manufacturer, while another might be a sugar refinery. A copper mining company might agree to sell its anticipated year's production of copper in advance, at an agreed-upon price, to a copper wire manufacturer.

Whenever a producer can budget its sales revenue ahead of time and a manufacturer can budget its future material costs, both entities can structure their operations more efficiently.

Eventually, speculators stepped into the commodities markets. A speculator would try to predict the future movement in a commodity's price and would buy or sell contracts *with no expectation of ever delivering or taking delivery of the specific commodity.* **Over time, speculation has overtaken the volume of trading by producers and consumers. Fortunes have been made and lost and** *free market prices have been manipulated.*

All commodities contracts have expiry dates on which the particular commodity must be delivered. Accordingly, prices can vary dramatically from one day to the next before and after an expiration date. Big money wins far more often than average small-time investors.

To deal with this inequity, I'd like to make a suggestion based on an important concept that applies to regulate the insurance industry.

Try to answer these questions. Can I legally take out a life insurance policy on *your* life, assuming you are *not* a family member or business partner? Can I buy fire insurance on your home with myself as beneficiary? The answer in both cases is NO! If I were able to do these things, I might be inclined to murder you or burn your house down (or both!).

To legally buy an insurance policy, the purchaser must possess what is called **"an insurable interest"**- *a*

valid reason for the purchase- whether it is life insurance or property insurance. I have an insurable interest in my spouse, children and home-but you don't.

My proposal, therefore, is to establish the legal concept of a "commodities interest" that would prohibit *anyone* who is not in the *business* of either producing or using a particular commodity from trading in it.

I would make an exception for gold and silver since many people hedge against possible declines in the value of paper currencies by purchasing these. **However, I would still disallow the sale of contracts that were not owned beforehand. In other words, the general prohibition that I have postulated against shorting stocks would apply to gold and silver too.**

Finally, let's look at options.

A financial option is the *right to buy or the right to sell* shares of a stock, bond, commodity, or any other investment instrument at some time in the future. There are various option terms generally spanning from one month to two years into the future.

For example, assume I am looking at the price of a (fictitious) company called Consolidated Widgets (CW). I think the price will double in six months but either I don't have enough money to buy lots of shares and/or I don't want to risk a big chunk of my capital if I'm wrong. Therefore, I could consider buying **"call"** options on CW at today's price (or some other price either higher or lower) exercisable in six month's time. If the price of CW rises, I can sell my option and pocket the difference between the market value at that time and my option price, minus the cost of the option itself. If the stock does not go up, all I will lose is the price of the **option**, which is usually small relative to the price of the actual stock. Buying options is an excellent strategy for many investors since the required investment is much less than buying the actual stock.

If I *already owned* CW stock and wanted to protect myself against a possible decline in value, I might buy **"put"** options that would guarantee me a minimum price, for example, six months later. This is often a good and acceptable strategy *–as long as I own the underlying investment in the first place and can deliver it.* If the stock drops, I can still get its earlier value and all I lose in the cost of the option, which becomes the equivalent of premiums paid on an *insurance policy.* In these circumstances, the option I have bought is called a "covered option", because my right to sell is "covered' by the fact that I already own the investment.

However, under the rules that apply within the current financial system, if I expect the price of CW shares to fall, I can buy **"put"** options on CW that give me the right to force someone else to buy CW shares from me in, say, six month's time-*even if I don't own the shares in the first place.* **If I have lots of money, nothing stops me from shorting the stock itself to artificially give my options value.**

Earlier, I made the strong recommendation that shorting of shares be completely outlawed. I now propose extending that recommendation to "put" options as well, *unless* the buyer owns the underlying investment

and is merely using the "put" as an insurance policy.

I recognize that many readers might view the proposals in this chapter as a major emasculation of the securities industry and as a major assault on our free-market system as it now operates.

They are right!

My point is that the greed that infests Unbridled Capitalism is threatening to cause the economic collapse of our nation. **Market manipulation must be halted.**

"We have met the enemy and he is us."

Pogo   Walt Kelly (1913-1973)

Question 35: **Do you agree that short selling of shares, bonds and other financial instruments traded on U.S. markets should be made illegal?**

Yes___ No___ Undecided___

Question 36: **Do you agree that U.S. Exchange Traded Funds (ETFs) should be prohibited from short selling investments and/or markets?**

Yes___ No___ Undecided___

Question 37: **Do you agree that financial institutions (both publicly and privately owned) should be assessed a 10% surtax on profits from day trading?**

Yes___ No___ Undecided___

Question 38: **Do you support the establishment of a legal concept called a "commodities interest" that would prohibit *anyone who is not in the business* of either producing or using a particular commodity (except gold and silver) from trading in it?**

Yes___ No___ Undecided___

Question 39: **Do you agree that selling gold and silver should be prohibited unless the seller is disposing of gold or silver that is already owned?**

Yes___ No___ Undecided___

Question 40: **Do you agree that buying "put" options should be made illegal unless the buyer owns the underlying investment and is using the put as an insurance policy against possible declines in value?**

Yes___ No___ Undecided___

CHAPTER 5
REFORMING BIG BUSINESS AND PENSION PLANS

I have been a Canadian Chartered Accountant for over 45 years and have held a U.S. CPA designation for the past 15 years. In all that time, I have witnessed amazing growth in technology. When I was an articling accounting student in 1964, my boss proudly showed me the firm's new Xerox machine but I was cautioned never to make too many copies with it since it was prone to catching on fire. In those days, financial statements were typed on onionskin paper – five copies at a time- with carbon paper in between each sheet. One last minute change or typing error required a total redo. (I won't share my experiences sharpening goose quill pens.)

When I matured and thought fleetingly of hanging out my own shingle, I often expressed the sentiment that I would rather have ten $3,000-a-year clients than one $30,000 client. *The larger the client, the harder it becomes to maintain independence.*

As you might expect, auditing public companies is much more difficult than dealing with family-owned businesses, although both present their challenges. In the 1980s, Sam Antar, who was later convicted of fraud, was chief financial officer of Crazy Eddie Inc., an electronics retailer that went public in 1983. Antar now teaches FBI agents about white-collar crime. In a recent interview, MarketWatch quoted him as follows:

"As a private company we understated income by skimming money to steal the sales tax and evade income taxes. As a public company we did the opposite: We overstated our income to sell stock at inflated prices.

The reason you do that is because as a public company you get a bigger bang for the buck by overstating income and overstating your taxes than understating income and understating taxes. That's because as a private company you are not trading stock. As a public company your stock trades at a multiple of earnings. Let's say I understate income by a million dollars, I may save $400,000 in taxes. But if I overstate my income by the same million dollars and overpay taxes by $400,000; that $600,000 in overstated net income, if the stock is trading at 30 times earnings, increases the value of the company by $18 million.

It is the economics of white-collar crime: Overpaying taxes and overstating income is better as a public company."

Over the years, many steps have been taken in the U.S. to guard against fraud. The Public Accountants Oversight Board now oversees the activities of public company auditors and regulates their responsibilities. Chief Executive Officers and Chief Financial Officers must sign off on their companies' financial statements and certify that they are not aware of any undisclosed fraud.

Nevertheless, some financial statement manipulation is unavoidable. If a company expects its next quarter to be weaker than the current one, it can easily defer making some large sales. If the current quarter looks a bit weak, it's easy to postpone some major costs, such as an advertising campaign. The media makes a big fuss over the fact that a particular company's earnings may have beaten analysts' estimates by a penny, or that a company may have had sales that were 2% lower than anticipated. The day traders have a field day when the market for that stock jumps or falters, while the small investor watches the gyrating stock price and is left shaking his or her head in frustration.

However, the real problem in assessing any investment in a publicly traded company stems from the complexities of the age in which we live.

There's an old joke where someone asks an experienced accountant, "How much is 1+1?" The accountant responds, "How much do you want it to be?"

In the olden days, auditing involved detailed testing of transactions. As the scope of business grew, such testing became prohibitively expensive. The emphasis gradually switched over to a review of a business's "internal control". These controls are measures that incorporate systems of checks and balances designed to deter mistakes, fraud and illegal acts. Effective controls are designed primarily through policies involving "division of labor".

For example, a business cannot have the same person who receives cash from customers also empowered to issue credits. If this lapse in control were allowed to happen, the employee could pocket cash and cover his or her tracks by writing off the customer's debt with a credit note.

Relying on a business's internal control has its limitations, although companies and their auditors are generally honest and well meaning. If a problem arises, it's usually because of one or two reasons.

First, an internal control system can be circumvented by collusion. If management really wants to commit fraud, it's not that difficult to overstate inventories or underestimate payables- especially if the scope of the business is international.

Secondly, *it's not the day-to-day ordinary transactions that often lead to fraud. It's the special, complex one-time deals that are sometimes kept off the books.* Enron is a good example.

No matter how knowledgeable the lead auditor(s) may be, the executives of a large company have the edge if they want to take it. **Overstating profits often leads to bigger bonuses and more valuable stock options.**

True, senior management must certify to the fairness of their company's financials. This gives the auditor some protection in the event of lawsuits, but this is not enough. **In my opinion, the only viable (although not perfect) way to virtually eliminate corporate fraud would be to administer lie detector tests to senior executives quarterly before financial information is released.**

Besides considering fraud, there are other financial and accounting issues that must be dealt with. The first is the *complexity of public company financial statements*. For example, the actual financial numbers of General Motors for the 2011 year were reported on **five pages**.

There were also 30 explanatory notes and additional required disclosures that were added on the next **50 pages** of the annual report. (Beyond the foregoing, I have never analyzed GM's numbers and all my comments that follow are generic.)

Often, important information is left off the financial statements and is buried in a company's notes, such as under-funding of pensions and certain contingencies. These are often referred to as "off-balance-sheet" items. Based on my experience, there are three major areas that need to be examined to make financial statements more reliable as an indicator of a business's financial position. They are:

1. Property, plant and equipment

2. Pension plan liabilities

3. Investments and loans

I will discuss the first two of these topics here and I will cover investments and loans in Chapter 6 –Reforming U.S. Banking.

The problem with the disclosure of property, plant and equipment is that Generally Accepted Accounting Principles **(GAAP)** mandate disclosure at **historical cost** (minus accumulated depreciation), *without reference to current market values*. This is because any disclosure methodology other than original costs involves *estimates*. While estimates can theoretically be manipulated, the use of **accredited independent valuators would minimize this problem**.

I can illustrate why a change to market value disclosure is needed with a few examples.

Many years ago, I was working in the Montreal Canada office of Touche Ross Chartered Accountants (now called Deloitte). I was given a thin file that contained two pieces of paper. The first was a corporate balance sheet. It showed an investment in land of $10,000 and a corresponding shareholders' equity of $10,000. I thought someone was playing a trick on me. "Who would hire a top-ranked accounting firm for this small a company?" I asked myself. Then, I looked at the second piece of paper, which was a memo from the senior tax partner in the office. It appeared that the land had been bought in the 1930s for $10,000 and was now worth over $1 Million. The original shareholders had passed away and their heirs wanted the company to sell the land and distribute the after-tax proceeds. My job was to calculate how much each shareholder would keep after both corporate and personal taxes were paid.

It became painfully obvious to me that any financial statement becomes meaningless if the numbers do not reflect *current values as determined by independent qualified appraisers*.

My second example is theoretical. Assume a corporation is formed to build a hotel at a cost of $1 Million and the operators/investors put up $250,000, while a lender finances $750,000. The projections for the hotel call for an anticipated average occupancy rate of 65%. Let's then assume that, after completion, the actual occupancy rate is 80%. It becomes obvious that the hotel is worth more than its cost and that the company's stock is therefore worth more. However, no attempt is made under current GAAP to adjust the numbers on the corporate balance sheet.

Conversely, assume there is an economic downturn and the occupancy rate drops to 35%. At that point, two things happen. First, the hotel would be worth a great deal less than its original cost to any prospective buyer. **Second, the collectibility of the loan would be in jeopardy.** *(This is an important concept in my next chapter on reforming U.S. banking.)*

Yes, one may argue that downturns tend to be temporary and that most markets are cyclical. However, no one can really define "temporary". Ironically, the valuation issue with which I am concerned is confined mainly to real estate and its related financing. By way of contrast, in mining and exploration, share prices fluctuate based on current commodity prices, which is a readily available benchmark. In manufacturing, property, plant and equipment values may not be affected by a downturn as long as the business's products are still likely to be in demand on the next upswing.

Another accounting valuation problem exists with respect to depreciation write-offs. Depreciation affects both the current year's net profit and the net value of property as reflected on the balance sheet. Depreciation is supposed to allocate the cost of property as a business expense over its useful life.

Again, I'll give you two examples why the current accounting system is flawed. The first pertains primarily to buildings in both the private and public (state and municipal governments) sectors and to infrastructure assets, such as bridges and roads primarily in the public sector.

It is customary to depreciate buildings over 30-50 years. I ask, "Why?" In many cases buildings *appreciate* over extended periods of time- as long as they are well maintained. **In the public sector, it is permissible under the accounting rules NOT to depreciate property as long as repairs are kept up to date. I suggest that similar rules be adopted within the private sector, although the main change that I believe is necessary, is the adoption of fair mark value disclosure principles. Historical depreciation calculations become irrelevant if fair market valuations are recorded and adjusted as necessary.**

My second example that illustrates why traditional accounting is flawed considers the issue of **depreciation estimates**. Accounting estimates are *not regulated* even though depreciation rates for income tax purposes are, of course, legislated.

Assume Anheuser-Busch (AB) and Miller-Coors (MC), the country's two largest breweries each buy $10 Million of *identical* beer brewing vats. AB anticipates that this equipment will have a useful life spread evenly over 10 years. The annual depreciation expense would therefore be $1 Million. On the other hand, what if MC assumes a useful life spread evenly over 20 years? MC's annual depreciation expense will only be $500,000. Assuming, hypothetically, that the two businesses are identical in all other respects, MC will appear to be twice as profitable as AB, since its depreciation expense would be half as large as that recorded by AB.

Of course, there are independent analysts as well as analysts employed by investment houses who sift through the numbers presented by publicly-traded companies and provide the rest of us with recommendations whether to buy, sell, or hold shares (or debt) of these companies. As I've already said, anyone who provides recommendations is supposed to disclose whether they own a position in a particular investment. But, I ask the rhetorical question, "Are these persons always unbiased?" If an analyst recommends a stock that his or her employer owns, could it be that the recommendation is made primarily to boost the share price so that the analyst's employer can then sell its holdings at a larger profit?

To summarize, I believe that there are major flaws in the generally accepted accounting methodologies for property, plant and equipment and related depreciation, I am therefore recommending several changes to the accounting disclosure rules that would make the system more transparent for non-professionals.

My first recommendation is that businesses should be required to reflect property, plant and equipment at fair market values on their financial statements, such values to be determined by qualified independent appraisers.

My second recommendation is that annual depreciation of property, plant and equipment, as reflected on a business's income statement, should also

be determined by qualified independent appraisers, taking into account industry norms, when appropriate to do so.

The last topic in this chapter is probably one of the most important topics in this book since it affects millions of Americans. It deals with pension plans and the need for you to take **an active role in planning for your retirement. I believe the material is worth reading carefully even if you aren't covered by a pension plan at work since it also deals with Individual Retirement Accounts (IRAs).**

Current tax rules in the U.S. permit **self-employed persons** with high incomes to contribute up to $51,000 annually, on a tax-deductible basis, into a retirement program called a Keogh plan. Self-employed persons with more moderate incomes can set up Self Employed Person Individual Retirement Accounts (SEP-IRAs) and make annual tax-deductible contributions of up to 20% of their business earnings. Thus, an accountant (?) who earns $100,000 annually from his or her practice can set aside up to $20,000 a year towards retirement. After taking into account the allowable tax deduction and resulting tax savings, his or her out-of-pocket cost is only around $13,000.

By way of contrast, if one is **employed**, the maximum annual contribution to an IRA is $5,000 ($6,000 if you are age 50 or older). This amount may be doubled if you are married, even if your spouse is not working. However, if either you or your spouse are members of an employer-sponsored pension plan, your right to use IRAs may be limited, depending on your income(s). In addition, **under current income tax legislation,** *you must either make your contribution for a given year on a current basis or lose it forever. There are no provisions to carry forward unused allowable contributions.*

In my opinion, the present U.S. income tax system virtually forces anyone who is not self-employed to seek work with an entity that provides a pension plan since the allowable contribution limits to IRAs are so much smaller than the generous allowances afforded to self-employed persons.

Here is how pension plans are structured.

A pension plan may be "contributory" or" non-contributory", depending on whether or not an *employee* is expected to contribute into the employer's plan. (In all cases, the employer must contribute.)

Pension plans may be divided into two types:
1. Defined contribution plans
2. Defined benefit plans

Under a **defined contribution plan**, the employer simply contributes a specified percentage of each employee's salary or wages each year and, if the plan is contributory, the employee also pays in with tax-deductible contributions withheld from his or her paycheck. The trustees of the plan invest all contributions. At retirement, whatever is accumulated for the benefit of the particular employee is extracted by the trustees, who must buy an annuity, *based on then-current rates of return,* guaranteed to provide the employee with a post-retirement income. If one is willing to accept a lower monthly payout, the annuity can be structured as a "joint and last survivor" annuity that will endure until both spouses die. One may also opt for a minimum guaranteed term payout even if the beneficiary dies prematurely.

Within a defined contribution plan, the *employee* assumes all the risk of inflation, poor investment performance, and low yield rates on annuities at the time of retirement.

You might be happy if you have been able to take advantage of low interest rates to buy or refinance a home. You might not have cared (until now) whether the stock market crashes, because you might have believed that only rich people lose money when there is a crash. **The point is, if you are a member of a pension plan *you do have a vested interest in the markets for stocks and bonds*.** While a home may be more affordable in a low interest rate environment, **your pension plan's performance is probably lagging**. If low rates become permanent, and/or if you are unlucky enough to retire in the midst of a severe downturn in the stock market, you will not be protected.

Let's now take a detailed look at defined benefit pension plans.

Under a **defined benefit pension plan**, the arrangement is designed to provide each employee with a post-retirement income computed with reference to both length of service and average annual salary over the few years preceding retirement. For example, an employer might use a benefit formula calling for a pension of "2% of the average of an employee's last three years' salary multiplied by the number of years of service."

For example, if the average of your last three years' salary is $60,000, and you will have been employed for 25 years, you might receive an initial annual pension of 50% (2% x 25 years) of $60,000, or $30,000 a year. In many cases, the initial payout is then indexed annually for inflation. If, at the time of retirement, your home is paid off and you have no dependent children to support, a pension of about half of your final earnings may very well be adequate to meet your post-retirement income needs-especially if your spouse or partner has income as well.

Where a defined benefit plan is in place, the *employer* assumes all the risk of inflation and poor investment performance.

Defined benefit plans are extremely popular in the *public sector*. If you are a municipal or state employee, work for the federal government or are a teacher, the chances are you are covered by a defined benefit pension plan. I believe that most long-term "public servants" have *grown complacent* in America and don't see the need to take control of their own finances.

However, there have been over 40 municipal bankruptcies in the last few years, with Detroit being

the largest and most recent (at the time this is being written). *Complacency is much overrated!*

Now let's look at the private sector.

According to a July, 2012 article in the New York Times, **338 of the Standard & Poor's 500 largest corporations in the U.S. have defined benefit pension plans for their employees.** *Only 18 are fully funded.* **Total under funding at the time that article was written amounted to $355 Billion.**

When a defined benefit plan is adopted, actuaries must take many factors into account in order to establish the required level of annual contributions. Many of these considerations are derived from statistical analysis, such as the percentage of employees who are likely to remain with the employer until retirement and how long they can be expected to live. Projections also have to be made with respect to anticipated salary and wage increases over time. **One of the most important calculations involves *a projection of future investment yields.***

If the actuaries employed by any entity, public or private, assume a long-term average yield of 6%, and, for a five or six-year period, the actual plan performance is, say, in the 2% range, *a shortfall in plan assets is inevitable.* Often, the shortfall faced by an employer's plan is hidden in the notes to the financial statements.

Recently, the U.S. government took steps to

artificially manipulate the extent of rampant under funding by allowing the projection of investment yields to be based on twenty-five year averages, instead of prevailing rates!

In May 2013, CNBC.com published an article on the Internet written by senior editor, Mark Koba. I am reproducing it here.

New Rule Signals Kiss of Death for Pensions

"A little-known rule change that allows companies to contribute fewer dollars to pension funds is signaling just how meaningless the retirement vehicle has become.

"This proves that pensions are pretty much dead," said Greg McBride, chief economist at Bankrate.com. "The change is just another charade to mask the under funding of pensions and increases the odds of having less money for retirement."

"It's not necessarily the immediate end of pensions but it's not good for them and it's certainly a bad sign," McBride added.

The pension change was part of a transportation bill—called Moving Ahead for Progress in the 21st Century or MAP-21—passed by Congress last June. The change became mandatory this year.

In essence, MAP-21 lets employers put less money in their pension plans by allowing them to value their liabilities— what they have to pay out to pensioners—using a 25-year average of interest rates instead of current rates.

When interest rates are low, like now, pension plan liabilities are estimated to be higher and companies have to put in more money. When rates are higher, the liabilities are figured to be smaller and employers' contributions are less. **The 25-year average is expected to be at least 2-3 percentage points higher than rates today.**

The reduced amount that companies will be putting in has to be figured out by each firm based on the higher rates. **But Madison Pension Services,** a consulting firm, has reported that **some minimum pension contributions in 2012 were reduced by 33 percent.**

Employers are not required to offer pension plans, but the government encourages them to do so by offering tax breaks. For 2012, **the tax subsidy for private and public retirement plans was $135.8 billion, the largest of all federal tax expenditures, according to the Pension Rights Center, a consumer advocacy group.**

But the number of workers with pensions has been on a steep decline. According to the **Bureau of Labor Statistics**, about 18 percent of full-time **private industry** workers had a defined pension benefit in 2011—down from 35 percent in 1990.

To end pension obligations and escape from having to keep throwing money into pensions that may be under funded, many firms, including **General Motors** and **Ford**, have offered lump-sum payouts to retirees.

"Companies want to get away from pensions totally," said Steve Pavlick, worker benefit specialist at the law firm McDermott Will & Emory.

"It's costing them a lot to come up with the cash to fund these plans and it's adversely affecting them, especially now with these lower rates," Pavlick said. "Most companies don't want to fund them in the future and aren't offering them anymore to new workers."

What's replaced pensions since the 1990s have been the employee contribution model like 401(k)s, which are now the main form of retirement plans offered to workers.

But pensions are still a key source of income for many current retirees, according to the Pension Rights Center. **The group said** that only 52 percent of seniors receive income from financial assets—and half of those seniors receive less than $1,260 a year from Wall Street.

And Social Security payments to retirees average only $15,179 a year, roughly two-fifths of their earnings before retirement.

The Pension Rights Center calls for more pension funding, not less.

"While the Pension Rights Center is sympathetic to business concerns, we believe that Congress must strike the right balance between giving employers a break on making pension contributions and protecting the pension fund and workers' and retirees' long term security," the group's executive vice President, Karen Friedman, **said on the center's website**.

Getting long-term pension security won't be easy. The government likes the current change as much as companies do.

Pension contributions are not taxed until benefits are paid to retired workers. **As such, the government is literally counting on money from the lower contributions by assuming it will get more tax revenues from higher wages of current workers—wages given instead of pension contributions.**

The MAP-21 rule on pensions is supposed to phase out, but Pavlick said plans are underway to get it or something like it extended.

"There's a lobbying effort to make this type of change permanent," he said. "It's clear that companies would rather have the higher interest rates and figure their pension contributions on such a plan."

While current pension holders seem likely to escape the fallout from the contribution cuts, analysts say future retirees with pensions will have to figure on fewer dollars.

"People getting pension checks this week or next month won't be affected," McBride said. "It's the young person of today that has to worry about getting full pension benefits when they retire."

While MAP-21 might not be a final nail in the coffin for nongovernmental pensions, experts say it does mean future retirees face an even tougher struggle to survive.

"Pensions are just not relevant anymore," said Pavlick. "Companies feel over regulated and can't afford them. In today's world, pensions are relics."

What I learned from this article is that, by allowing pension plans to calculate what their projected liabilities *would be* if yields were *several percentage points higher than their actual earnings,* our government has permitted 338 out of America's 500 largest corporations to legally cook their books!

If I were to go to my bank, and ask for a loan, my banker would ask me for details about my income. What if I answered, "Well, I made $30,000 last year but *if* I had gotten a raise *of 6% a year for the last 5 years, my income would now be around $40,000."*

I recommend that pension plans should be abolished, while the existing IRA provisions should be expanded. Once again, Enlightened Capitalism embraces the concept of *social responsibility.* Even if we are not super-wealthy, I believe *we must all take primary responsibility for our own retirement planning.* We should not be relying on any employer, public or private, to do all our thinking for us.

If pension plans are to be terminated, I suggest that the assets should allocated fairly among the different classes of participants in the following order:

1. Former employees who have already retired
2. Employees age 55-65 who are willing to take early retirement
3. Employees age 55-65 who will be maintaining their employment
4. Employees age 45-55

5. Employees age 35-45
6. Employees under age 35

Each group would be required to share in any shortfall, with younger employees assuming the major portion of the total deficiency since, as a group, they would have more time to recoup their losses.

I also recommend that each beneficiary's distribution should be allowed to flow without any current taxation into a personal IRA. Each person would generally be prohibited from making withdrawals until age 59 ½, as is now the case. I would also like to see employers be required to provide and pay for up to two hours of investment consulting advice through independent firms, so that employees could tailor their own IRA plans to suit their individual circumstances.

In addition to the forgoing, I believe that a realistic formula to expand IRA limits should be introduced that could be indexed from time-to-time:

1. **There should be a mandatory annual employer contribution to each employee's IRA of 8% of salaries and wages to an annual maximum of $10,000 (8% x $125,000). ***

2. **Each employee should be permitted to match his or her employer's contribution in *whole or in part*, generally by way of deductions withheld from paychecks. The employee's contribution could be made into**

either a regular IRA or a Roth IRA ** at the employee's request

3. Employee contributions to a regular IRA should be tax deductible. *In addition, all of the employee's contributions should qualify for a 25% tax credit.* (The deduction would essentially refund 25% of the average employee's contribution, assuming an average Federal tax bracket of 25%, and the 25% tax credit would reduce his or her final out-of-pocket cost to only half the contribution.)

4. The "use it or lose it" tax rules should be repealed. Any eligible amount not contributed by an employee in a given year should be available for an unlimited carry forward to any subsequent year. This provision would take into account the fact that a family's ability to save increases once their home is paid and there are no longer any dependent children living at home.

*According to an Internet site called *MyBudget360. com*, only 20.8% of American households earn $100,000 or more annually and only about 60% of these make over $150,000. My best guess is that only 10%- 12% of *individuals* earn more than $125,000. It is true that, in a few cases, there are two high-income-earners in the same household and the rules I have suggested would provide a larger benefit than if one person earned $250,000. However, this anomaly is probably not all that relevant and is not worth over-complicating the Tax Code.

** In a Roth IRA, the contributions are not tax-deductible, but the eventual payouts after retirement are not taxable. Roth IRAs are popular among younger people who are in lower tax brackets, don't really need tax deductions, and who want to take advantage of the option to earn long-term tax-free income within their plans rather than only tax-deferred income.

Let's take a look at a "quick and dirty" calculation showing how such a program such as the one I am recommending could work:

Assume an employee is now 40 years old and expects to retire at age 65.
Assume a current salary of $40,000 and an **average salary increase of 3%***.
The employee's final salary is mathematically projected to be $84,000.
Average annual salary is approximately $40,000 + $84,000/ 2 = $62,000
Average annual employer contribution to the employee's IRA 8% x $62,000=$4,960
Assume the employee matches this contribution.

Note: Employee's cost;

Outlay:	$4,960
Tax savings 25%:	(1,240)
Tax credit 25%:	(1,240)
Annual out-of pocket cost:	
	$2,480

(Approximately $200 a month)

Average annual total IRA contribution $4,960 + $4,960= $9,920

Assumed average annual yield **4%***

The total amount in the IRA at age 65 is projected mathematically to be $413,000

Estimated annual annuity yield –joint and last survivor, guaranteed for 15 years- is approximately $22,300.

(I consulted some recent annuity tables. The payout will be about $450 per month for each $100,000 invested. So, $450 x 4.13 x 12 = $23, 302 per annum.)

*Obviously, no one can realistically project either average wage increases or investment yields over 25 years. In this example, the annuity is just over 25% of the employee's final earnings. That doesn't seem too exciting. However, consider the following:

1. The difference between $84,000 and $22,300 is significantly less than $61,700 *after taxes.*

2.   This example does not take the post-retirement income of a spouse or partner   into account.

3.   Social Security is not accounted for.

4.   If the employee's primary residence is mortgage-free at retirement and there are no dependent children in the household, the cost of living could theoretically be less in future dollars than it is in today's dollars.

Postscript: Below is a MarketWatch article by Retirement Columnist Robert Powell entitled "Will your pension disappear, post-Detroit" which appeared the day I wrote this chapter (July 24,2013).

"State and local government workers with traditional pension plans might want to revisit their retirement-income plans in the wake of Detroit's filing for bankruptcy.

As many know by now, workers and retirees for that troubled city, which has an under funded pension liability of some $3.5 billion, face the possibility that their pensions could be reduced drastically in a worst-case scenario.

A hearing to determine whether a lawsuit by the city's 20,000-plus retired public employees can block the bankruptcy is scheduled. But no matter what happens, experts say that now would be a good time for public-sector workers and retirees—especially those whose employers have under funded pensions—to revisit their retirement plan, crunch out a few what-if scenarios, and adjust their current or planned lifestyle accordingly.

Despite their having earned their benefits through years of employment, alarming headlines are shaking current and future retirees' confidence in their retirement security," said Richard Schroder, President of Anova Consulting Group, a Brookline, Mass., market research and consulting firm focused on the retirement-services space.

According to published reports, public pensions aren't the only ones in trouble. The Teamsters' Central States, Southeast & Southwest Pension Plan, which is the nation's largest multi-employer pension fund, faces tough times, too. Documents filed at the end of 2012 by the Rosemont, Ill.-based fund show that its liabilities are almost double its assets — $34.9 billion versus $17.8 billion, according to a recent BenefitsPro report,

Detroit's bankruptcy and the under funded status of the Teamsters' pension are only the latest examples of an age of increasing uncertainty for Americans planning for retirement,

Schroder said.

Create a worst-case plan

"Now more than ever, it is incumbent upon Americans to take increased responsibility for their personal financial well-being," Schroder said. "At one point or another, most of us have been given the advice to 'not put all our eggs in one basket,' and the same concept applies to retirement."

Schroder said worst-case "what-if" scenarios, such as the prospect of pension benefits being reduced, should be considered as part of retirement planning. He also said most Americans would be well served by improving their financial literacy or having discussions with a qualified financial adviser.

What's an appropriate worst-case scenario? Consider the case of Central Falls, R.I.: After declaring bankruptcy in 2011, that city slashed one in three of its retirees' pension checks by more than half, with the majority of the city's former public-safety workers set to lose tens of thousands of dollars a year, according to published reports. The former acting fire chief's pension dropped by $41,684 a year, from $75,789 to $34,105; a former firefighter's pension dropped by $37,628, from $68,414 to $30,786; and a former policeman's pension dropped by $36,493, from $66,351 to $29,858.

Given that example, part of your worst-case scenario planning should be to envision how you'd get by if your expected pension were cut in half. That should give you a sense of whether you could live on the reduced pension, or whether you might need to bump up your savings rate, or delay retirement, or return to work, or reduce your standard of living, or any combination of those actions.

"Individually, each person may not be able to affect the outcome around her respective pension reform," said Jeffrey Tomaneng, a financial adviser at Lincoln Investment Planning. "However, he or she does have the ability to control expectations and make adjustments to lifestyle and budget."

From the planner's view, Tomaneng said, you still use the same fundamentals of the financial-planning process. "You still discuss worst-case, best-case and variations of in-between scenarios," he said. "Spend less, earn more, save more, work longer, retire somewhere cheaper and so forth."

Tomaneng noted that in Massachusetts former Polaroid employees, in the wake of that company's bankruptcy, are already receiving payments from the federal Pension Benefit Guaranty Corp. (PBGC) at a fraction of what they were supposed to receive. "Many have delayed their retirements and cut back on their lifestyles to give them a better shot of making sure they don't outlive their money," he said.

Tomaneng said he's also been addressing with younger clients the possibility of reduced benefits from Social Security. "For these union workers and retirees the discussion and planning needs to happen right away," he said.

Is your pension funded?

Americans would also be well-served to check the degree to which their pension plan is funded.

Indeed, some cities and states are much worse off than others. For instance, in 2010, Joshua Rauh, a professor of finance at Stanford University, and Robert Novy-Marx, an associate professor of finance at the University of Rochester, identified the **10 major cities** that they calculated would be the first to run out of pension-fund money. **At the time, that list included Philadelphia; Chicago; Boston; Cincinnati; St. Paul; Jacksonville, Fla.; New York City; Baltimore; Detroit; and Fort Worth.**

Meanwhile, the gap between the promises states have made for public employees' retirement benefits and the money they have set aside to pay these bills was at least $1.38 trillion in fiscal year 2010, according to the Pew Center for the States' analysis of pension and retiree health-care funding. According to the report, Connecticut, Illinois, Kentucky and Rhode Island were the worst among the states, with pensions under funded 55% in 2010. Pew also noted that states collectively had only 5% of the funds needed to pay for their retirees' health care and other non-pension benefits—such as life insurance. And 17 states had not set aside any money to fund their retiree health-care liabilities.

Others agreed that it's important to check the financial status of your pension plan. **"Any type of plan participant, public, private, or union should always keep an eye out on the financial status of their employer,"** said Ary Rosenbaum, an ERISA retirement plan attorney for his firm, The Rosenbaum Law Firm.

Rosenbaum noted that union plans and private pensions offer more safety to plan participants when it comes to providing information, because plan participants have a right to access their plan's funding notice, which can tell them how under funded their plans are. If their plan is covered by the PBGC and funding of the pension is less than 80%, then plan participants are required to receive a notice of the plan's funding level. But the PBGC doesn't cover most state and local public-sector pension plans.

"Plan participants should know that whether their plans are protected by the PBGC or not, there is always a risk that their pension benefits can be curtailed by bankruptcy court as what probably will happen to City of Detroit pensioners," said Rosenbaum. "So they should plan accordingly."

No need to push panic button?

Some experts don't think that all current and retired state and local government workers need to push the panic button and redo their retirement plans.

Notwithstanding a few outliers, retirement benefits for the vast majority of the more than 8 million retired employees of state and local government are safe and secure, said Keith Brainerd, the research director of the National Association of State Retirement Administrators, a nonprofit association whose members include the directors of many of the nation's state- and territorial-level public retirement systems.

As of March 31, 2013, for instance, combined assets of these funds exceeded $3.5 trillion, more than 15 times what the funds pay out each year in benefits, he said. What's more, Brainard said, these plans collect in employee and employer contributions each year much of the amount they pay in benefits.

There are undoubtedly some public plans in trouble, and some in serious trouble, such as those in the state of Illinois, Brainard said. Yet nearly every state has made changes to their retirement plans since 2009, some more than once. A number of states, including Colorado, Minnesota, Maine, South Dakota, Rhode Island and New Jersey, have reduced their unfunded liabilities, in part or in whole by reducing future cost-of-living adjustments (COLAs) for current retirees. In addition, many states have increased required contributions for employees, including current workers in many cases.

In the cases of Detroit and Central Falls, Brainard said a distinguishing feature is the decline in revenue those cities experienced. Reading between the lines, **if you currently work for or are retired from a municipality where revenues are declining and there haven't been changes made to the pension plan, consider working on your plan-B retirement strategy**.

Because retiree health-care benefits generally have far fewer legal protections than pension benefits do, Brainard said, we are likely to see more reductions in those benefits than among pensions.

Bottom line: When it comes to your pension, leave nothing to chance. Create a just-in-case plan. Prepare for the worst and hope for the best."

Question 41: **Do you agree that senior executives of public companies be required to take polygraph (lie detector) tests quarterly before financial information is released in order to minimize fraud risk?**

Yes___ No___ Undecided___

Question 42: **Do you agree that businesses should be required to reflect property, plant and equipment at fair market values on their financial statements, such values to be determined by qualified independent appraisers?**

Yes___ No___ Undecided___

Question 43: **Do you agree that annual depreciation of property, plant and equipment should be determined by qualified independent appraisers, taking into account industry norms, when appropriate to do so?**

Yes___ No___ Undecided___

Question 44: **Do you are that pension plans should be required to calculate over or under funding annually with reference to *current* investment yield rates instead of 25-year averages?**

Yes___ No___ Undecided___

Question 45: **Do you agree that all pension plans should be wound up with assets being distributed (without taxation before eventual withdrawal) to Individual Retirement Accounts (IRAs) of retirees and employees in an equitable manner with reference to current ages?**

Yes___ No___ Undecided___

Question 46: **Do you agree that, instead of having pension plans, employers should contribute annually to the personal IRAs of employees?**

Yes___ No___ Undecided___

Question 47: **Do you agree that a mandatory annual employer IRA contribution of 8% of salaries and wages to a maximum of $10,000 appears reasonable as a starting point?**

Yes___ No___ Undecided___

Questions 48-50 should be considered together:

Question 48: **Do you agree that employees should be permitted to match employer contributions to an IRA in whole or in part? (Employees may split their contributions between a regular and a Roth IRA.)**

Yes___ No___ Undecided___

Question 49: ***In addition to the available tax deduction
for regular IRA contributions, do you agree with the
proposal that a 25% tax credit also be allowed, in
order to reduce the average employee's after-tax cost
of contributing to about 50% of total contributions?***

Yes___ No___ Undecided___

Question 50: **Do you agree that the "use it or lose it rules"
should be repealed and that any eligible amount not
contributed by an employee to an IRA in a given year
should be available for an unlimited carry forward to
any subsequent year?**

Yes___ No___ Undecided___

CHAPTER 6
REFORMING U.S. BANKING

I'd like to begin this chapter by explaining the circumstances that lead to the U.S. banking crisis that began in 2008 and which is still, in my opinion, very much with us today. If something is to be reformed, I believe it is necessary to first pinpoint the flaws that must be eliminated.

Let's go back a few years and pretend that you are thinking about making an interest-bearing investment, instead of entrusting your money to the vagaries of the stock market. An investment advisor tells you that he or she can find a first mortgage for you to invest in that will yield 7 ½ % a year, with interest paid monthly. The borrowers have bought a home with a 25% down payment and a major bank has loaned them the rest of the purchase price after checking their credit. The bank is now willing to sell the mortgage to you.

You ask your advisor, "Why does the bank want to sell the mortgage?" The advisor answers, "It's because the bank makes hefty fees from writing mortgages and it pays them to sell these mortgages to investors in order to free up lending capital for new mortgage deals." You ask your advisor to give you some time to think.

A few days later, the advisor calls and tells you about a brand new option which he or she refers to as a "mortgage-based *derivative*". He or she explains that, "*A derivative is simply an investment that is derived from something else.* In this case, the investment is a *share in a bundle of mortgages* that have been *combined into a single package.* Instead of forcing an investor to put all of his or her eggs into one proverbial basket- a single mortgage-, the derivative investment provides an opportunity to participate in *a **mortgage portfolio*** that *spreads the risk of loss among a large number of investors.* If one borrower stops paying, the rest of the portfolio would still be performing. In fact, if foreclosure proceedings were instituted against the delinquent and the property were sold, there might even be a windfall profit for the investors!"

You ask the advisor, "So, what's the catch?" The advisor answers, "There isn't any except the yield is only 6 ½ % because of the fees charged by the lending institutions for packaging and selling these ***mortgage-backed securities***. That's what they're called. The thing is," the advisor concludes, "I believe it's worth sacrificing 1% of your potential yield for the opportunity to hedge your bets and spread your risk." Again, you ask for a day or two before making any decision.

Two days later, your advisor calls and says, "There's now a terrific new refinement to this mortgage-backed security program I've been telling you about. There's this giant reputable insurance company that's willing to *insure the entire portfolio* for a small fee. Your yield drops by a half of one percent to 6%- but it's a *totally risk –free investment!*" "I'm in," you reply. "In fact, get me $75,000 of these mortgage whatevers instead of the 50 grand we discussed before!"

Now, let's turn to the banks and the other institutions that were in the mortgage-lending business at that time. In the early years of this century, after the Dot com collapse began to recede from memory, lenders were conducting business as usual and making normal mortgage loans to qualified borrowers.

Then, someone somewhere came up with a brilliant idea. That person saw that writing mortgages produced big fees, while keeping them on the books meant tying up capital for (perhaps) many years, often at relatively fixed rates. This nameless genius (I'm not being facetious- really!) then came up with the idea of **packaging** these mortgages and selling **mortgage-backed securities** to investors. Doing so would then free up lending capital for new mortgage underwritings that would generate additional fees.

The idea of bundling mortgages for sale to investors caught on, especially when (presumably) some other genius (again-really!) in the insurance industry came up with the idea of **insuring these mortgage-backed securities against loss**.

Truly, both of these concepts -packaging and insurance- were brilliant ideas. **However, both were predicated on the maintaining of sound lending practices.**

Enter the greed of Unbridled Capitalism.

Banks and other lenders quickly came to the conclusion that, *if they weren't going to keep newly-written mortgages on their books, it really made very little difference to them whether the borrowers had decent credit and/or the ability to repay their debts.*

They began to offer financing for home purchases to everyone and their dogs.

The loosening of credit quickly started to balloon into a housing bubble as more and more families bought into the Great American Dream. As demand for housing grew, prices rapidly began to escalate. Many people began to believe that they could conceivably buy homes on speculation using borrowed money *without ever making any payments at all.* They would simply sell before foreclosure actions could be taken and their expectation was often a 10%-20% profit on sale. **Other people were mesmerized by the tax deductibility of home mortgage interest, which, as you will see, is a clear case of the tail wagging the dog.**

Here's a true story. At the time all this was going on, the wife of a friend of mine was thinking of buying a duplex as an investment. She had no job and no money. A mortgage broker told her to state on her application that she was employed as a nanny and was paid $50,000 a year under the table. She was told that no one would check. Fortunately, she didn't buy.

A detail that I haven't mentioned so far pertains to an important feature of many of the insurance arrangements for these mortgage-backed security portfolios. Sometimes, lenders were actually able to arrange insurance on a ***non-recourse*** basis. That meant that, if the portfolio went bad, the insurance company could not come back to the original lenders and force them to absorb all or part of the losses. At other times, lenders insured mortgages on a ***full-recourse basis,*** which meant that, if the mortgages went into default, the lenders would take them back. Both insurers and lenders were thus exposed to risk of loss.

The housing bubble grew so large, that it is quite possible that some lenders actually hoped that borrowers would default, thereby allowing them to repossess properties that could then be resold at a profit.

Well, we all know what happened. The bubble burst, housing prices dropped, and many homeowners found themselves caught up in the **Great American Nightmare**.

People whose debts exceeded the now-depleted values of their homes abandoned them and lenders began to foreclose.

Traditionally, before the crash, America's banks were required to maintain capital (let's call it "equity) equal to around 10% of their assets and investments. This means that 90% of assets and investments could legitimately be financed with monies borrowed from depositors and other sources. **If the value of a particular bank's assets dropped by more than 10%, that bank would become insolvent.** Bank failures did occur from time-to-time, but they certainly weren't commonplace. All that changed in 2008.

To the extent that insurance companies insured mortgage-backed securities without recourse, they became liable for impaired or uncollectible mortgages. The largest casualty was American International group (AIG). The banks themselves also suffered staggering losses and their shoddy lending practices have come back to haunt them to this day. There are still outstanding lawsuits involving billions of dollars in claims.

Then came the Great American Bailouts.

Today, the U.S. government would like us all to think that the problems have all been solved, but this is not the case. The banks that survived are simply feeding foreclosures into the marketplace slowly to forestall panic by depositors. The proof is that it takes months for offers on foreclosed properties to be accepted. **This is because acceptance means that shortfalls would have to be recognized as losses on the banks' books.**

Here's the worst! In the last chapter, I explained how the government has been able to artificially permit pension plans to understate their funding deficiencies by allowing then to calculate projected yields on invested funds based on 25-year average returns rather than actual. Well, what I'm about to tell you trumps this blatant regard of responsible accounting.

For over twenty years, generally accepted accounting principles (GAAP) required entities to **value loans and other investments at market values when reporting, rather than at cost.** This was and is called the **"mark-to-market"** rule.

However, when the banking crisis hit, the government forced the Financial Accounting Standards Board to modify the mark-to-market rules in cases where no "orderly" market (a relatively equal number of buyers and sellers) exists and/or it is likely that loans and advances will be "held to maturity". *This gave America's lending institutions the right to defer the recognition of their losses and to mask their insolvency.* I am not aware of any objections made by the American Institute of Certified Public Accountants.

By relying on official pronouncements rather than common sense, the "independent" auditing firms are now free to issue annual reports stating that the financial statements of these institutions "present fairly" their financial positions and the results of their operations. No write-downs to recognize extraordinary losses is necessary!

If you are interested, I have copied below excerpts from a Wikipedia article on "mark-to-market" accounting. (It is not required reading. There is no test for you to worry about.)

"**Mark-to-market** or **fair value accounting** refers to accounting for the "fair value" of an asset or liability based on the current market price, or for similar assets and liabilities, or based on another objectively assessed "fair" value. Fair value accounting has been a part of Generally Accepted Accounting Principles (GAAP) in the United States since the early 1990s, and is now regarded as the "gold standard" in some circles.

Mark-to-market accounting can change values on the balance sheet as market conditions change. In contrast, historical cost accounting, based on the past transactions, is simpler, more stable, and easier to perform, **but does not represent current market value. It summarizes past transactions instead. Mark-to-market accounting can become inaccurate if market prices fluctuate greatly or change unpredictably. Buyers and sellers may claim a number of specific instances when this is the case, including inability to value the future income and expenses both accurately and collectively, often due to unreliable information, or over-optimistic or over-pessimistic expectations.**

As the practice of marking to market became more used by corporations and banks, some of them seem to have discovered that this was a tempting way to commit accounting fraud, **especially when the market price could not be determined objectively (because there was no real day-to-day market available or the asset value was derived from other traded commodities, such as crude oil futures)**, so assets were being 'marked to model' in a hypothetical or synthetic manner using **estimated valuations** derived from financial modeling, and **sometimes marked in a manipulative manner to achieve spurious valuations. The most infamous use of mark-to-market in this way was the Enron scandal.**

After the Enron scandal changes were made to the mark to market method by the Sarbanes–Oxley Act during 2002. The Act affected mark to market by forcing companies to implement stricter accounting standards. The stricter standards included more explicit financial reporting, stronger internal controls to prevent and identify fraud, and auditor independence. In addition, the Public Company Accounting Oversight Board (PCAOB) was created by the Securities and Exchange Commission (SEC) for the purpose of overseeing audits. The Sarbanes-Oxley Act also implemented harsher penalties for fraud, such as enhanced prison sentences, and fines for committing fraud. Although the law was created to restore investor confidence the cost of implementing the regulations caused many companies to avoid registering on stock exchanges in the United States.

As the practice of marking to market became more used by corporations and banks, some of them seem to have discovered that this was a tempting way to commit accounting fraud, especially when the market price could not be determined objectively (because there was no real day-to-day market available or the asset value was derived from other traded commodities, such as crude oil futures), so assets were being 'marked to model' in a hypothetical or synthetic manner using estimated valuations derived from financial modeling, and sometimes marked in a manipulative manner to achieve spurious valuations. The most infamous use of mark-to-market in this way was the Enron scandal.

Problems can occur when the market-based measurement does not accurately represent the underlying asset's true value. **This can occur when a company is forced to calculate the selling price of these assets or liabilities during *unfavorable or volatile times*, such as a financial crisis.** For example, if the liquidity is low or investors are fearful, the current selling price of a bank's assets could be much less than the value under normal liquidity conditions. The result would be a lowered shareholders' equity. **This case occurred during the financial crisis of 2008/09 where many securities held on banks' balance sheets could not be valued efficiently as the markets had disappeared from them. During April 2009, however, the Financial Accounting Standards Board (FASB) voted on and approved new guidelines that would allow for the valuation to be based on a price that *would be received in an orderly market* rather than a forced liquidation, starting during the first quarter of 2009.**

The SEC and the FASB issued a joint clarification regarding the implementation of fair value accounting in cases where a market is disorderly or inactive. This guidance clarifies that forced liquidations are not indicative of fair value, as this is not an "orderly" transaction. Further, **it clarifies that estimates of fair value can be made using the expected cash flows from such instruments,** provided that the estimates represent adjustments that a willing buyer would make, such as adjustments for default and liquidity risks.

Opponents argue that the implications for investors are that the valuation of assets underlying such securities will be

**increasingly difficult to analyze, not less so. An example would
be determining a company's actual assets, equity and earnings,
which will be overstated if the assets are not allowed to be
marked down appropriately."**

As an aside, valuations of pension plan liabilities
and bank assets are not the only areas where reported
financial information is manipulated. As you probably
know, the measure of market health most heavily touted
on a day-to-day basis by the financial media is the Dow
Jones Industrial Index. This index tracks the movement of
thirty of America's biggest companies listed either on the
New York stock Exchange or the NASDAQ. What many
people don't know is that if a particular company slumps
badly (sometimes as a result of an entire sector falling out
of favor), it is dumped from the list and replaced. In recent
years, General Motors, Citigroup, American International
Group (the largest insurer of mortgage-backed securities)
and Kodak were removed. **Removal and replacement by
thriving businesses keeps the index at artificially high
levels.**

I believe that, for now, U.S. financial institutions
have learned their lesson-**perhaps too well.** From recent
personal experience, I have found it difficult to get bank
financing. When I decided to move to the U.S. full-time, I
put my home in Canada on the market. I sold my smaller
second home in Palm Desert and bought a larger one for
cash.

When my Canadian home didn't sell as quickly as I
expected, I found that I needed a $75,000 temporary loan.
Because I didn't want to take money out of my retirement
fund, I tried to get a Home Equity Loan. I was able to prove

my income and my net worth with no problem. I owned the home free-and-clear and the requested financing was only about **15% of market value.**

Unfortunately, my credit rating was impaired because of a collection action for $30,000 filed against me by a hospital. I explained that the matter was under litigation and that it would probably be settled without any out-of-pocket cost to me (which it was six months later).

Nevertheless, the banks I went to for a loan turned me down. One of them was Bank of America where I have held a credit card with a $25,000 limit for thirteen years. I sometimes have run up monthly charges of $7000-$8,000, but I always pay in full before the due date. To the best of my recollection, I have never been charged even one-cent of interest. When I applied, I was told, "Sorry, the only factor that matters to our loan department is your credit scores."

When I requested copies of these scores, I found out that I had "lost" brownie points not only because of the legal issue, but also because, in someone's opinion, I was using too much credit on a monthly basis. It made not a whit of difference that I paid all my bills in full monthly and had no delinquencies.

A friend of mine later told me that I should always pay my bills a week or so before I get my statements to reduce the balances reported to the credit bureaus. (You can do this quite easily as long as you can track your credit card balances on-line.)

Another "problem" I was faced with, was that the

credit bureaus disclosed they were receiving "too many requests" from lenders for credit reports on me. Hello!! What would anyone expect if they were shopping for financing? The fact that I did not actually incur any debt never entered into the equation. (Once the collection issue was resolved, I got my financing.)

I believe that banks should be required to place less reliance on credit reports and more reliance on *people*, their financial positions and their collateral. To me, that's the **"Enlightened"** thing to do. I miss the days when branch managers were permitted to make decisions without having to forward their files on to nameless faces at head offices.

Before I suggest a method to alleviate the ongoing banking crisis, I'd like to tell you one more story. I lived in Montreal, Canada from 1956 until 1977. At the age of 33, I moved to Calgary, Alberta, where I took a teaching position at the University of Calgary. The week I arrived, I made an appointment with the manager of the closest branch of The Royal Bank of Canada. I introduced myself and told him a bit about what I did for a living. I explained that I didn't need any money, but simply wanted to arrange an **unsecured** line of credit for any contingencies that could arise. I told him that I had had such a credit line for $25,000 with the Royal in Montreal. (This is probably the equivalent to about $100,000 today.) The manager gave me a three-word reply: "You've got it!" Talk about the good old days….

O.K. Back to the present. So far, I've hammered lending institutions and government agencies. Now it's time to consider all of us- the American public at large. I'd like to introduce the topic of **responsible borrowing**.

One of the biggest injustices perpetrated by the U.S. tax system is the over-generous deductibility of home mortgage interest. The current tax rules allow interest to be deducted on up **to $1 Million dollars of total financing with respect to not one, but *two* homes!** I call this an "injustice" because these tax rules foster **irresponsible borrowing**.

Even in times of low interest, if you're in the top tax bracket, you must still pay over 60% of the interest (and all of the principal) with after-tax dollars. It's worse if you are in a lower tax bracket and the deduction saves you less.

Two Homes? What are they thinking? Over 65% of households lived in their own homes before the 2008-2009 crash. I couldn't find any statistics on multiple home ownership, but I'd expect it's a great deal lower than 65%. Who are the people who own multiple homes? Frankly, I don't expect an answer-it's too obvious.

To encourage responsible borrowing and fairness, I recommend the following:

1. **The Internal Revenue Code should be amended to restrict the deductibility of home mortgage interest (and property taxes) to costs incurred with respect to only ONE owner-occupied primary residence.**

2. **The maximum debt that qualifies for deductibility of interest should be limited to**

THREE TIMES the adjusted gross income of the person or persons (in case a joint return is filed) who are claiming the deduction.

3. **The overall qualifying home mortgage debt limit on which interest is tax-deductible should be reduced from $1 Million to $500,000.**

I also recommend two further changes.

4. **While interest on credit card debt and (personal-use) automobile loans is not deductible, there is a tax provision whereby homeowners can deduct interest on up to $100,000 of "Home Equity Lines of Credit' (HELOCS). In order to foster responsible borrowing, I recommend that the deductibility of such interest be restricted to situations where the loan proceeds are used for *structural home additions and improvements*. Prospective borrowers would be required to present project proposals to lenders, along with quotations from contactors and suppliers, before financing could be secured. In addition, upon completion, copies of invoices from the trades would be required for lenders' files.**

5. **To qualify for home mortgage interest deductibility, mortgage terms should be limited to *fifteen years*. If a home mortgage is refinanced, to retain tax deductibility, the maximum term of the refinancing should be limited to fifteen years minus the term that has already elapsed since the initial mortgage**

financing was granted.

I strongly believe that our tax system must encourage Americans to reduce their mortgage terms to fifteen years. The problem is that *the conventional term of thirty years is just too long*! My primary rule governing effective financial planning is **NEVER ENTER RETIREMENT WITHOUT A FULLY PAID HOME. You do not want to be making mortgage payments out of post-retirement income.** Moreover, as we have seen in our daily lives, people are often encouraged (or forced) to retire in their fifties. If both spouses or partners are working to support themselves and their family, one spouse may die or become disabled. Making ongoing mortgage payments on a smaller income can then become an insurmountable challenge. *A family's best insurance policy is a short-term mortgage.*

In Canada, for example, mortgage interest on a personal residence is not tax- deductible. Nor are property taxes or loans for home improvements. When the financial crisis hit in the U.S., Canada and its banks survived relatively unscathed. In general, outside of Toronto and Vancouver, Canadian house prices have always tended to be significantly lower than those in the U.S. **In the U.S., mortgage interest deductibility has had an inflationary effect on house prices** because of what I have referred to as overly generous tax deductions. Take a look at the example below:

	United States	Canada
Mortgage principal	$100,000	$70,000
Assumed interest rate	5%	5%
First year's interest (approximate)	$5,000	$3,500
Tax saving	$1,500	$1,500
Owner's assumed tax bracket	30%	Irrelevant
Tax saving	$1,500	None
Net out of pocket cost	$3,500	$3,500

If an American can afford to borrow an extra $30,000 compared to a Canadian, it is likely that the American would be willing to pay more for a comparable home.

The next table is the really important one. If this is new to you, please study it carefully. The table calculates the difference between fifteen year financing and thirty year financing of $100,000 at a 5% mortgage rate. (If your outstanding mortgage is, for example, $213,000, just multiply the numbers below by 2.13.)

	Thirty Year Mortgage	Fifteen Year Mortgage
Mortgage principal	$100,000	$100,000
Interest Rate	5%	5%
Monthly Payment	$536.82	$790.79
difference of:	$253.97	
Total payments	$193,256	$142,342
difference of	$50,914	

| Total Interest | $93,256 | $42,342 |
| difference of | $50,914 | |

The above example shows how, for approximately an extra $250 a month for every $100,000 of financing, you can pay for your home fifteen years earlier, enhance your financial security, and save almost $51,000. For a while, the extra $250 may mean going out for dinner less lavishly or frequently, bringing your lunch to work, having an after-work drink at home instead of at the neighborhood bar, or choosing a less expensive car to drive.

When I taught at the University of Calgary, I gave an annual evening lecture called "Year-end Tax Planning for Faculty and Staff." The cost was $10 per person and the proceeds went to a scholarship fund for business students. To my initial amazement, I soon discovered that the wealthiest people on campus were **the janitors**. At the time, most of them were European immigrants. They saved their money and invested in real estate.

I realize that, for many Americans, buying *and keeping* a home is a stretch, even if a family is willing to cut back on discretionary costs such as eating out or is willing to make do with a cheaper car. If a breadwinner is unemployed *or underemployed*, shelling out an extra $250 a month may represent an insurmountable obstacle.

However, my Doctrine of Enlightened Capitalism is really an *integrated plan* in which all the pieces must fit together to solve one big jigsaw puzzle.

For example, if you currently work for a large corporation where senior executives take home millions of dollars each year and these executives were now required to "share the wealth" as I recommended earlier, you would certainly be able to afford accelerated mortgage payments.

If the thousands of jobs that have been shipped overseas were brought back, an equal number of Americans would no longer be either unemployed or underemployed.

The changes I have recommended and will be proposing won't ever happen by themselves. As a nation, we must conquer general apathy and elect a government that represents *all* our interests.

In concluding this chapter, I'd like to present a plan that I believe would eliminate most of the residue of the banking crisis that still hangs over the U.S. today.

I was personally very much opposed to the extensiveness of the 2008-2009 bank bailouts. No doubt, some government assistance was necessary, but I believe that our leaders missed the proverbial boat. **My idea at that time was to bail out *homeowners*- not the banks.** I sent my recommendations to a number of financial commentators in the hope that they would be disseminated to the public, but I got no replies whatsoever. Although much damage has since been done from forcing people out of their homes, I believe the ideas that follow still have merit.

1. **In cases where people are "upside down" on their mortgages, I suggest that they should be allowed to *remain in their homes* subject to the following conditions:**

- **They should be offered 15 year fixed-rate financing at an interest rate of 5% on a principal amount of *75%* of the balance owing to the institution that holds the particular mortgage.**

- **The remaining debt (25%) should be *deferred without interest for up to fifteen years.* If the homeowners and/or their immediate family are still living in the home at that time, this debt should then be forgiven (without any adverse income tax consequences).**

- **In the event that the home is sold before the fifteen-year period elapses, the deferred 25% amount of the original debt would become due and payable, along with the then outstanding balance of the 75% refinancing.**

Here's my thinking. To the extent that people faced with the threat of foreclosure accept this arrangement, the banks will then have *performing* loans of 75% of the amount that is now on their books. In addition, housing markets are cyclical. In many cases, one might expect a significant improvement some time within the next fifteen years.

People often move for various reasons. Often, a move is the result of a job change. Sometimes, a family's income grows and they upgrade to a more expensive home. In other cases, the choice is to downsize. It is impossible to provide any estimates, **but I believe that, in a significant**

number of cases, people would sell their homes before the fifteen year deferral period is over and the lending institution will be paid off in full.

Everyone wins!

2. **In cases where foreclosed homes are empty, I suggest that prospective purchasers be offered similar incentives so that the remainder of most foreclosed properties can be removed from the books of lending institutions. To ensure that buyers act in good faith, I suggest a required down payment of 10% of the outstanding debt owing on the property. The lender would then provide fifteen-year fixed financing at 5% for 75% of the purchase price. *The remaining 15% of the property's cost would be deferred and forgiven in equal annual installments of one-fifteenth each year. If the property is sold after seven and one-half years, 50% of the deferred amount would become due and payable out of the proceeds of sale.***

Again, 75% of the "bad" loans would now become performing loans. The only potential loss would be 15% (after buyers' down payments). For the reasons I've already given, many buyers will sell before the full fifteen years have elapsed and actual write-offs by lenders will likely be fairly minimal.

A program such as this one would be easy to administer since the numbers would be readily determined and there would be no negotiation. The only issues would be whether buyers have the necessary down payment, whether they qualify for the required financing and whether they would accept the terms of the deferral/forgiveness of debt.

Question 51: **Do you agree that the Internal Revenue Code should be amended to restrict the deductibility of home mortgage interest (and property taxes) to these costs incurred with respect to only ONE owner-occupied home?**

Agree___ Disagree____ Undecided____

Question 52: **Do you agree that the maximum debt that qualifies for interest deductibility should be limited to THREE TIMES the adjusted gross income of the person or persons (in case a joint return is filed) who are claiming the deduction?**

Agree___ Disagree___ Undecided___

Question 53: **Do you agree that the maximum qualified debt limit on which interest is tax-deductible should be reduced from $1 million to $500,000?**

Agree___ Disagree___ Undecided___

Question 54: **Do you agree that that the deductibility of interest on a Home Equity Line of Credit (HELOC) should be restricted to situations where the loan proceeds are used for *structural home additions and improvements*?**

Agree___ Disagree___ Undecided___

Question 55: **Do you agree that, to qualify for home mortgage interest deductibility, mortgage terms should be limited to *fifteen years*, and, if a home mortgage is refinanced, to retain deductibility, the maximum term of the refinancing should be limited to fifteen years minus the term that has elapsed since the initial mortgage financing was granted?**

Agree___ Disagree___ Undecided____

Question 56: **Do you agree that, in cases where people are "upside down" on their mortgages, they should be allowed to remain in their homes subject to the following conditions?**

They should be offered 15 year fixed financing at an interest rate of 5% on a principal amount of 75% of the amount owing to the institution that holds the particular mortgage.

\-   The remaining debt should be *deferred without interest for up to fifteen years.* If the homeowners and/or their immediate family are still living in the home at that time, this debt would then be *forgiven* (without any adverse income tax consequences).

\-   In the event that the home is sold before the fifteen-year period elapses, the deferred 25% amount of the original debt would become due and payable, along with the outstanding balance of the 75% refinancing?

Agree___ Disagree___ Undecided___

Question 57: **Do you agree that, in cases where foreclosed homes are empty, prospective purchasers should be offered incentives to buy them and, to ensure that buyers act in good faith, they should be required to make a down payment of 10% of the outstanding debt owing on the property; the lender would then provide fifteen-year fixed financing at 5% for 75% of the purchase price and *the remaining 15% would be deferred and forgiven in equal annual installments of one-fifteenth each year?***

Agree___ Disagree___ Undecided___

CHAPTER 7
REFORMING THE U.S. HEALTHCARE SYSTEM

"The only thing we have to fear is fear itself"

- FDR, 1932

"The only thing we have to fear is an uninsured medical issue"

- Anonymous, 2013

The pitiful waste that permeates the U.S. healthcare system is one of the main reasons I decided to write this book.

I am very disappointed that Obamacare does not mirror the benefits of socialized medicine as it operates in many countries, including our neighbor to the North. From 2003 until 2012, my primary residence was in Victoria, British Columbia. My monthly B.C. Healthcare premium was about $100 for family coverage. Single coverage runs about $60 per month. Prescriptions are not covered except for low-income seniors and other people whose incomes are substandard. However, Canadian prescription costs are about 60% of what I now pay as a resident of

California, even after senior and insurance discounts. Eye care examinations are covered in Canada for children and seniors. Normal dental work is not, but employers often offer dental insurance.

To the best of my knowledge, *not one country that has adopted socialized medicine has ever reverted to a U.S.-based model.* Now that the USA's credit rating has been downgraded by Standard & Poor, ALL the <u>remaining</u> AAA-rated nations all have some kind of socialized health care. They are:

- <u>Australia</u>

- <u>Austria</u>

- <u>Canada</u>

- <u>Denmark</u>

- <u>Finland</u>

- <u>France</u>

- <u>Germany</u>

- <u>Guernsey</u>

- <u>Hong Kong</u>

- <u>Isle of Man</u>

- <u>Liechtenstein</u>

- <u>Luxembourg</u>

- <u>Netherlands</u>

- <u>Norway</u>

- <u>Singapore</u>

- <u>Sweden</u>

- <u>Switzerland</u>

- <u>United Kingdom</u>

Here are some interesting statistics. All of the countries in this chart have socialized healthcare **except the U.S. and Japan**. The chart is extracted from a Wikipedia article on healthcare in Canada

Country	Life Expectancy	Physicians per 1000 people	Nurses per 1000 people	Per capita expenditure on health	Healthcare costs as a percent of GDP	% of government revenue spent on health	% of health costs paid by government
Australia	81.4	2.8	9.7	3,137	8.7	17.7	67.7
Canada	81.3	2.2	9.0	3,895	10.1	16.7	69.8
France	81.0	3.4	7.7	3,601	11.0	14.2	79.0
Germany	79.8	3.5	9.9	3,588	10.4	17.6	76.9
Japan	82.6	2.1	9.4	2,581	8.1	16.8	81.3
Sweden	81.0	3.6	10.8	3,323	9.1	13.6	81.7
UK	81.0	2.5	10.0	2,992	8.4	15.8	81.7
US	78.1	2.4	10.6	7,290	16.0	18.5	45.4

Many Americans have problems with the concept of "**socialized** medicine." As I've stated before, **Americans must stop equating social responsibility with Communism. The system I am advocating is Enlightened** *Capitalism. Please reserve your judgment until you've read this entire chapter.*

In some instances, the countries that embrace socialized medicine have programs administered by the government. In Canada, the different provinces run their own programs. There is reciprocity so that, if someone lives in Ontario and falls ill in British Columbia, their Ontario plan will foot the bill. In Switzerland, I gather that there are 92 private company insurers. Healthcare is not as cheap as in Canada and according to an article I read on nation.time.com, adults pay an average of $300 a month. There are some co-pays, but no one pays more than 8% of annual income.

I hope my point is clear. ***Americans must stop viewing socialized medicine as a Communist plot.***

Now let's address the issue of patient **satisfaction**. It is really difficult to obtain reliable data on this subject. Many Americans have been led to believe that the Canadian system is flawed. They make reference to "long wait times" and the "fact" that "hordes" of Canadians flock to the U.S. for procedures such as knee and hip replacements.

From personal experience, I can tell you that this is an overstatement.

Emergency medical care in Canada is excellent. It is true that one might have to wait for certain non-life-threatening procedures, but the waits tend to be reasonable. If one is wealthy, he or she may decide to go to the United States for certain surgeries, but I think this is relatively rare.

If the U.S. adopts a system of providing socialized healthcare, I believe there is little danger of Americans experiencing wait times that are longer than what is acceptable. **The reason is that there are many more Physician Assistants in the U. S. compared to Canada.** While both countries have approximately 2.5 doctors for every one thousand inhabitants, the U.S has a much greater number of Certified Physician Assistants (PAs).

In Canada, there are presently only four PA educational programs, compared to 173 in the United States. According to the Physician Assistant Certification Council of Canada, there are currently only 396 accredited members. The American Academy of Physician Assistants, has, by way of contrast, over 90,000 members. PAs, for example, free up orthopedic surgeons so that they can handle far more non-life-threatening procedures, such as knee and hip replacements than their Canadian counterparts over the course of a workweek.

The next excerpt from Wikipedia describes the Canadian healthcare system and deals with the issue of how it is received.

"**Health care in Canada** is delivered through a publicly funded health care system, which is mostly free at the point of use and has most services provided by **private entities**. It is guided by the provisions of the Canada Health Act of 1984. The government assures the quality of care through **federal standards**. **The government does not participate in day-to-day care or collect any information about an individual's health, which remains confidential between a person and his or her physician.** Canada's provincially based Medicare systems are cost-effective partly because of their administrative simplicity. **In each province each doctor handles the insurance claim against the provincial insurer. There is no need for the person who accesses health care to be involved in billing and reclaim. Private health expenditure accounts for 30% of health care financing.**

Competitive practices such as advertising are kept to a minimum, thus maximizing the percentage of revenues that go directly towards care. In general, costs are paid through funding from income taxes. In British Columbia, taxation-based funding is supplemented by a fixed monthly premium, which is waived or reduced for those on low incomes. There are no deductibles on basic health care and co-pays are extremely low or non-existent (supplemental insurance such as Fair Pharmacare may have deductibles, depending on income).

The Provincial Ministry of Health issues a health card to each individual who enrolls for the program and **everyone receives the same level of care. There is no need for a variety of plans because virtually all essential basic care is covered, including maternity and infertility problems. Depending on the province, dental and vision care may not be covered but are often insured by employers through private companies. In some provinces, private supplemental plans are available for those who desire private rooms if they are hospitalized. Cosmetic surgery and some forms of elective surgery are not considered essential care and are generally not covered. These can be paid out-of-pocket or through private insurers.** *Health coverage is not affected by loss or change of jobs, health care cannot be denied due to unpaid premiums (in BC), and there are no lifetime limits or exclusions for pre-existing conditions.*

Pharmaceutical medications are covered by public funds for the elderly or indigent, or through employment-based private insurance. **Drug prices are negotiated with suppliers by the federal government to control costs. Family physicians (often known as general practitioners or GPs in Canada) are chosen by individuals.** If a patient wishes to see a specialist or is counseled to see a specialist, a referral can be made by a GP. **Preventive**

care and early detection are considered important and yearly checkups are encouraged. Early detection extends life expectancy and quality of life, and also reduces overall costs.

Public opinion

Canadians strongly support the health system's public rather than for-profit private basis, and a 2009 poll by Nanos Research found 86.2% of Canadians surveyed supported or strongly supported "public solutions to make our public health care stronger." **A Strategic Counsel survey found 91% of Canadians prefer their healthcare system instead of a U.S. style system. Plus 70% of Canadians rated their system as working either "well" or "very well".**

A 2009 Harris/Decima poll found 82% of Canadians preferred their healthcare system to the one in the United States, more than ten times as many as the 8% stating a preference for a US-style health care system for Canada **while a Strategic Counsel survey in 2008 found 91% of Canadians preferring their healthcare system to that of the U.S.**

A 2003 Gallup poll found 25% of Americans are either "very" or "somewhat" satisfied with "the availability of affordable healthcare in the nation", versus 50% of those in the UK and 57% of Canadians. Those "very dissatisfied" made up 44% of Americans, 25% of respondents of Britons, and 17% of Canadians. Regarding quality, 48% of Americans, 52% of Canadians, and 42% of Britons say they are satisfied.

Economics

In Canada, most services are provided by the private sector. **Each province may opt out, though none currently do.** Canada's system is known as a *single payer system*, where basic services are provided by private doctors (since 2002 they have been allowed to incorporate), with the entire fee paid for by the government at the same rate. Most government funding (94%) comes from the provincial level. **Most family doctors receive a fee per visit. These rates are negotiated**

between the provincial governments and the province's medical associations, usually on an annual basis. Pharmaceutical costs are set at a global median by government price controls.

Hospital care is delivered by publicly funded hospitals in Canada. Most of the public hospitals, each of which are independent institutions incorporated under provincial Corporations Acts, are required by law to operate within their budget. Amalgamation of hospitals in the 1990s has reduced competition between hospitals.

Wait times

Health Canada, a federal department, publishes a series of surveys of the health care system in Canada based on Canadians' first-hand experiences of the health care system.

Although life-threatening cases are dealt with immediately, some services needed are non-urgent and patients are seen at the next-available appointment in their local chosen facility.

The median wait time in Canada to see a special physician is a little over four weeks with 89.5% waiting fewer than 90 days.

The median wait time for diagnostic services such as MRI and CAT scans is two weeks with 86.4% waiting fewer than 90 days.

The median wait time for surgery is four weeks with 82.2% waiting fewer than 90 days."

Another study by the Commonwealth Fund found that 57% of Canadians reported waiting 30 days (4 weeks) or more to see a specialist, broadly in line with the current official statistics. A quarter (24%) of all Canadians waited 4 hours or more in the emergency room.

Since 2002, the Canadian government has invested $5.5 billion to decrease wait times. In April 2007, Prime Minister Stephen Harper announced that all ten provinces and three territories would establish patient wait times guarantees by 2010. Canadians would be guaranteed timely access to health care in at least one of the following priority areas, prioritized by each province: cancer care, hip and knee replacement, cardiac care, diagnostic imaging, cataract surgeries or primary care.

Canadians visiting the US to receive health care

Some residents of Canada travel to the United States for care. A study by Barer, et al., indicates that the majority of Canadians who seek health care in the U.S. **are already there for other reasons, including business travel or vacations. A smaller proportion seek care in the U.S. for reasons of confidentiality, including abortions, mental illness, substance abuse, and other problems that they may not wish to divulge to their local physician, family, or employer.**

In a Canadian National Population Health Survey of 17,276 Canadian residents, it was reported that 0.5% sought medical care in the US in the previous year. Of these, less than a quarter had traveled to the U.S. expressly to get that care.

A 2002 study by Katz, Cardiff, et al., reported the number of Canadians using U.S. services to be "barely detectible relative to the use of care by Canadians at home" and that the results "do not support the widespread perception that Canadian residents seek care extensively in the United States."

US citizens visiting Canada to receive health care

Some US citizens travel to Canada for health-care related reasons:

Many US citizens purchase prescription drugs from Canada, either over the Internet or by traveling there to buy them in person, because prescription drug prices in Canada are substantially lower than prescription drug prices in the United States; **this cross-border purchasing has been estimated at $1 billion annually**.

Because medical marijuana is legal in Canada but illegal in most of the US, many US citizens suffering from cancer, AIDS, multiple sclerosis, and glaucoma have traveled to Canada for medical treatment.

Now, let's examine the **concept of continuing to involve private insurance companies in the healthcare system** as proposed under Obamacare.

There are two serious flaws in the "old system" that Obamacare would perpetuate. First, **insurance companies are motivated by profit**. *To the extent that healthcare costs are "grossed up" to include these profits, Americans would continue to overpay by substantial amounts.*

A few years ago, I was confined to a California hospital for two days. The bill came to $60,000. When the hospital found out that my insurance claim was denied, they dropped the charge to $28,000. It took 2 ½ years, but I settled the bill for $12,000!

Then there is the fact that the whole process of billing a whole host of insurance companies creates an **administrative nightmare for doctors and hospitals**. Each provider, whether doctor, hospital or clinic, must create an infrastructure to handle billings. They must monitor collections and invoice patients for deductibles, co-pays and percentages of costs that are not covered. They must deal with patients (like me) who whine, cry and beg for reduced charges when fees are not covered by insurance.

Unfortunately, the insurance lobby is huge and powerful. Woe to any politician today who proposes limiting the scope of their activities! I have already recommended that lobbyists be prohibited by law from making any monetary payments to persons in government and/or to those who wish to ascend to high office.

If insurance companies continue to be mandated as the lynchpins behind our healthcare system, I believe our government is doing us grievous harm.

There are those who are opposed to Obamacare because they don't want to change the current system. They believe that each of us should make our own decisions whether or not to buy insurance. If no changes were contemplated at all, I think most insurance companies would be happy with the status quo.

The problem is that, maintaining the old rules, perpetuates Unbridled Capitalism. The insurance companies prosper and our elected officials enrich themselves at our expense.

This is NOT social responsibility. Many people in America live in fear of illness or accident. A great many uninsured people can't afford to obtain preventative care. Some are uninsurable or must pay hefty premiums because of pre-existing conditions.

Then there are many young people who believe they do not need health insurance. After all, they are invincible, aren't they? But, if the you-know-what hits the proverbial fan, they either have to rely on family assistance or face bankruptcy, unless they are fortunate enough to be employed at a job where health insurance is provided.

I firmly advocate a nation-wide system that closely follows the Canadian model since the two nations already share so many similarities. If the U.S. system were streamlined, and the federal (or state) government collected monthly premiums and paid out all essential medical costs, there is no reason to expect anyone to pay more than what one pays on average in Canada, i.e. $60- $100 a month. Low income Americans/ families would be exempt from paying premiums but would still be covered.

I would now like to address the **exorbitant cost of medical malpractice insurance in the United States.** My thesis is that, if doctors and hospitals paid less for their malpractice insurance, the general public would benefit from fee reductions, with no corresponding drop in **net** physician or hospital revenue.

Doctors and hospital administrators all live in fear

of malpractice lawsuits. I have seen and heard about practitioners ordering extra tests that may not really be required just to protect themselves from malpractice claims. I have had doctors admit to me that excess testing is the norm and not the exception. **If the medical malpractice threat can be reasonably curtailed, the entire U.S. healthcare system would function much more cost effectively.**

In law, there are two kinds of negligence. The first equates to a normal mistake and is referred to as "ordinary" negligence. We all make mistakes. They are an unavoidable component of life. The other kind of negligence is called "gross negligence". In the world of professionals, this means doing or (not doing) something that perhaps 95% of all practitioners would do (or not do). Gross negligence is also relevant if a professional performs badly while impaired.

I'm quite familiar with these concepts as they relate to the accountancy profession since I teach this material to would-be CPAs. I am not a doctor, but I think I can provide reasonable examples of gross negligence. Obviously, these include situations where the professional is drunk or under the influence of drugs- even certain prescription medications- that might impair his or her ability to function normally.

I'd expect a knee replacement procedure on the wrong knee would also be inexcusable. However, what if an accident victim who is barely conscious is brought into emergency, suffering great pain? He or she is administered a dose of morphine to alleviate suffering but succumbs to anaphylactic shock due to a rare morphine allergy. Should the family be permitted to sue a well-meaning physician for negligence? I think not.

Below is an extract from an article on malpractice costs in the United States written for ehow.com by Alexis Writing. You will see that, **in some cases, a physician's**

malpractice insurance may cost more than the average American earns in a year.

*"Medical malpractice insurance costs are rising yearly. Because of this, many doctors in various specialties are keenly aware of the laws and regulations that govern malpractice insurance, which vary by state. **A doctor will sometimes choose a state in which to practice based on malpractice insurance costs.** The averages vary dramatically by state, so a brief overview of states is necessary in order to get an indication as to how much a doctor can expect to pay.*

Variations between States

The average cost of medical malpractice insurance varies by state. There are a number of different factors that create these variations. Each individual insurer sets its own premiums for medical malpractice insurance, and these are based on incidents of litigation and other general assessments of the risk pool. This means the insurance companies providing insurance within the state look at the potential for lawsuits within that state, within that branch of medicine, and set insurance rates.

Differences among Specialties

Different specialties have different average costs because of varying levels of risk and the history of past litigation within those specialists. For instance, obstetrics has a very high rate of litigation. Damages also tend to be high when an infant is harmed at birth, because that infant will have to deal with that injury for its entire lifetime. The more potential for things to go wrong as a result of medical negligence, the higher the average insurance rates tend to be within that specialty.

Low Cost States

Minnesota has some of the lowest malpractice costs for doctors. However, the cost of insurance in Minnesota varies widely by specialty. Internal medicine, general surgery and obstetrics are three of the areas monitored by groups such as the Government Accountability Office. As of 2009, the average cost for malpractice insurance for general surgeons hovered around $10,000 per year; for internal medicine, $4,000 per year; and for OB/GYNs, up to $17,000 per year.

Malpractice liability insurance rates in California, on the other hand, depend largely upon demographics, so average rates may vary from place to place. Some of the largest insurers also deviate from one another widely in terms of how much insurance costs. At the low end, doctors in internal medicine may only pay $6,000 per year from premium coverage. **However, in 2009, OB/GYNs could end up paying more than $55,000 per year for insurance coverage. Insurance for general surgeons can cost between $22,000 per year and $34,000 per year.**

Average Cost States

Pennsylvania malpractice insurance falls in the middle with respect to average cost. Rates differ between the major insurers due to demographic and claims differences. In 2009, base rates for general surgery could be as low as $28,000 annually or as high as $50,000. Internal medicine malpractice insurance costs varied between $6,000 and $11,000. **Obstetricians/gynecologists could find themselves paying up to $64,000 or more for coverage.**

High Cost States

While Nevada malpractice insurance rates are between middle to high in comparison with all other states, doctors of many types in Nevada--including general internists, pediatricians and general practice doctors--earn a higher average salary than doctors in any other state. In 2009, one of the highest rates of insurance in Nevada is for OB/GYNs, who may pay between $85,000 for malpractice liability insurance per year up to $142,000 per year for a premium plan by a prominent insurance company. Although the average annual salary for such doctors was around $180,000 in 2009, malpractice insurance can still be a huge financial burden.

Florida has some of the highest rates of liability insurance. Moreover, the deviation between low and high averages varies in Florida more widely than in almost any other state. For instance, **a doctor in internal medicine in Florida could expect to pay in excess of $56,000 per year for insurance as of 2009, in contrast with Minnesota's $4,000. General surgeons paid in between $90,000 per year and $175,000 per year or more. OB/GYNs once again could expect the highest rates, with liability coverage ranging from $100,000 to $200,000 per year."**

Besides the fact that Canada has essentially restricted the role of insurance companies within its healthcare system to providing dental and prescription coverage, Canada has also introduced legislation to limit malpractice litigation.

Obviously, if the U.S. government were to take similar steps, *in the interest of social responsibility,* our politicians would have to ignore efforts by the legal profession to hang on to a very large cash cow. Clearly, however, if doctors no longer had to operate (pun intended) under the daily threat of malpractice suits, and if they didn't require the kind of fee structure needed to defray exorbitant malpractice insurance costs, they could deliver their services to all Americans at much reduced rates.

Below are extracts from a United States Library of Congress article entitled **"Medical Malpractice Liability: Canada".**

"Executive Summary

Canada has a single-payer health insurance scheme that covers virtually all residents. Most physicians are in private practice and they bill the insurance plans for their services. Being in private practice, they require medical liability insurance. This is usually obtained through a professional organization. However, physicians are reimbursed for a large portion of their insurance premiums by provincial governments. Fees are lower than in the United States for a number of reasons. Two of these are that Canada's highest courts have set limits on awards and the country's liability laws make establishing professional negligence more difficult. Another is that the physicians' insurance company defends lawsuits very vigorously.

Although Canada is often characterized as a country that has "socialized" medicine, its system differs considerably from countries in which physicians are essentially employed by the state or the entire medical profession is under unified state control. In Canada, most medical practitioners are in private practice just as they are in the United States. Most physicians have their own offices, set their own schedules, and see patients who have chosen to come to them on a regular basis or for a particular condition. Canadians are **not** assigned doctors by the government or an insurance plan. They do have choices.

Liability Insurance

Canadian physicians who are in private practice or work for hospitals are required to obtain medical liability insurance. Such insurance is available through the Canadian Medical Protective Association (CMPA). Insurance premiums or "membership fees" are based upon the type of work a physician performs and the region in which he or she practices. The three fee regions are Quebec, Ontario, and the Rest of Canada. The CMPA has published Fee Schedules. **Fees are not based upon a physician's record and are not increased for a history of complaints or on account of claims paid.**

Membership fees paid to the CMPA give physicians' insurance coverage and a right to representation in medical malpractice lawsuits. However, provincial governments reimburse physicians for at least a portion of their membership fees. These arrangements are not generally made public. However, a ...released Memorandum of Understanding between the Ministry of Health, the Ontario Medical Association, and the CMPA reveals that physicians are currently reimbursed for about 83 percent of their membership fees. It has been reported that the Ontario government paid about Can$112 million to reimburse physicians for medical malpractice fees in 2008.

Government officials in Ontario have explained that the purpose of the reimbursement program is to encourage physicians to practice in the province and not to move to another province or the United States where average incomes may be higher.

Critics contend that because the CMPA's fees are not based upon a physician's record, the system does little to penalize physicians who are found to be liable for malpractice even on multiple occasions. **Physicians who have committed acts of malpractice may, however, be disciplined by their provincial licensing body. Discipline can range from suspensions to losses of the privilege to continue practicing medicine.**

The CMPA has also been criticized for defending medical malpractice suits extremely vigorously and turning down reasonable offers to settle claims to discourage other lawsuits on a number of occasions. One judge reportedly referred to the CMPA as pursuing a "scorched earth policy."

In Canada, a losing party is generally required to pay about two-thirds of a successful party's legal fees. Since the CMPA often incurs large legal expenses in defending claims, this is an additional disincentive to persons who believe that they have been injured through malpractice from bringing an action for damages.

One other feature of Canadian law that tends to discourage parties from suing physicians for malpractice is that **the Supreme Court has set out guidelines that effectively cap awards for pain and suffering in all but exceptional cases.** In a trilogy of decisions released in 1978, the Supreme Court established a limit of Can. $100,000 on general damages for non-pecuniary losses such as pain and suffering, loss of amenities and enjoyment of life, and loss of life expectancy.

The Supreme Court did state that there may be extraordinary circumstances in which this amount could be exceeded, and courts have allowed the figure to be indexed for inflation so that the current suggested upper limit on awards for non-pecuniary (non-monetary) losses is close to $300,000.

Nevertheless, the flexible cap on non-pecuniary losses is a major disincentive to persons considering whether they should sue a physician for malpractice and for lawyers to specialize in or seek out malpractice cases.

The Supreme Court of Canada has also limited the types of cases in which punitive damages may be awarded, although it has allowed as much as Can$1 million in punitive damages in an extraordinary case. A Canadian law firm has summarized the holding in this leading case concerning punitive damages as follows:

Punitive damages are very much the exception rather than the rule:

-Imposed only if there has been high-handed, malicious, arbitrary or highly reprehensible misconduct that departs to a marked degree from ordinary standards of decent behavior.

-Where they are awarded, punitive damages should be assessed in an amount reasonably proportionate to such factors as the harm caused, the degree of the misconduct, the relative vulnerability of the plaintiff and any advantage or profit gained by the defendant,

-Having regard to any other fines or penalties suffered by the defendant for the misconduct in question.

-Punitive damages are generally given only where the misconduct would otherwise be unpunished or where other penalties are or are likely to be inadequate to achieve the objectives of retribution, deterrence and denunciation.

-Their purpose is not to compensate the plaintiff, but to give a defendant his or her just desert (retribution), to deter the defendant and others from similar misconduct in the future (deterrence), and to mark the community's collective condemnation (denunciation) of what has happened.

-Punitive damages are awarded only where compensatory damages, which to some extent are punitive, are insufficient to accomplish these objectives, and they are given an amount that is no greater than necessary to rationally accomplish their purpose.

-While normally the state would be the recipient of any fine or penalty for misconduct, the plaintiff will keep punitive damages as a "windfall" in addition to compensatory damages.

-Judges and juries in our system have usually found that moderate awards of punitive damages, which inevitably carry a stigma in the broader community, are generally sufficient.

Thus, punitive damages in tort actions in Canada are relatively rare.

Negligence

Despite the above factors that discourage medical malpractice lawsuits in Canada, there are numerous reported cases in which doctors, hospitals, and health care professionals have been found liable for acts of negligence in the delivery of health care. **In order to be successful, a plaintiff must show that the defendant owed him or her a duty of care, the defendant did not deliver the standard of care owed, the plaintiff's injuries were reasonably foreseeable, and the defendant's breach of the duty of care was the proximate cause of the plaintiff's injuries.** *An error of judgment is not necessarily negligence even if it causes injury.*

Common types of negligence actions are as follows:

> Failure to attend a patient
> Failures in diagnosis
> Failures in re-diagnosis
> Failures in referral or consultation
> Failure to communicate with other physicians
> Failure to protect or warn third parties
> Failure to report abuse
> Substandard treatment

Hospitals can be held liable under the doctrines of vicarious liability or direct liability for the conduct of their staffs."

To summarize the major points that I have raised so far:

1. The adoption of socialized medicine does not mean embracing Communism.
2. The issue of patient satisfaction under socialized medicine should not be blown out of proportion. *If problems, such as extended delays in providing*

treatment arise, they can be addressed as required.
The prevalence of trained Physician Assistants in
the U.S. will help greatly in reducing wait times.

3. **An effective healthcare framework cannot exist if profit-motivated insurance companies are an integral component of the system.**

4. **For a healthcare system to be effective, malpractice claims and awards must be regulated to protect physicians and reduce malpractice insurance costs that are of necessity passed on to patients.**

My next point is:

5. An effective health care system must not erode our employment base.

Below is an extract from an article written by Sean Williams for *The Motley Fool*, a well-known financial Internet site, entitled "*5 Ways Obamacare Will Fail*". This extract deals with the requirement that employers pay for coverage for full-time employees. Mr. Williams makes the argument that **under Obamacare, America runs the very real risk of becoming a nation of part-time workers. This issue is the first of his five concerns and I agree with his assessment:**

"**Obamacare will encourage job and R&D (research & development) outsourcing, as well as domestic hourly cutbacks.** This could be perhaps the most visible and negative immediate impact of Obamacare -- the outsourcing of American jobs and research and development, as well as the hourly cutbacks associated with the higher costs of providing subsidized group coverage.

In the health care sector, the reaction has been decisive and swift. **Stryker** (NYSE: SYK) , a maker of medical devices, implants, and supplies, shed 5% of its workforce because of the impact of the 2.3% medical device excise tax in a move expected to save the company $100 million annually. Keep in mind, this isn't an after-profits tax; it's 2.3% off a company's top-line revenue figure that goes directly to pay for the Medicaid expansion. The world's largest medical device maker, **Medtronic** (NYSE: MDT), is another perfect example. **It announced its intentions to hire up to 1,500 people last year, but commented that the majority of hires would be in markets abroad, like China.**

But, the truly dangerous aspect of Obamacare is that its outsourcing and hour-cutting aspects aren't just limited to the health care sector. For some large corporations, the cost of supplying subsidized health coverage to its employees versus cutting back their hours to part-time status and avoiding that requirement altogether is simply too great. In January 2013, 11 franchised **Wendy's** (NASDAQ: WEN) locations in Nebraska cut back hours for about 300 non-management employees in an effort to save costs since part-time employees are not required to be covered under the patient Protection and Affordable care Act.. Unfortunately, this isn't -- and won't be -- the only instance of this, and could negatively impact hourly employees' wages, as well as their potential to obtain health coverage."

In his Article, **Mr. Williams brings up, as his second concern, the potential issue that the medical system under Obamacare would be overloaded by an influx of new patients.** Here is what he says:

"Hospitals and physicians will be overwhelmed with the influx of millions of newly insured people.

There's a give and a take with every situation. Yesterday I proposed that *one of the greatest benefits of Obamacare is that it will open up the opportunity for previously uninsured or underinsured persons to get regular preventative care screenings. The downside of this scenario is that it will absolutely overwhelm our current health-care network.*

In 1996-1997, 46,965 first-time and multi-time applicants applied to medical school, according to data from U.S. Medical Students and Applicants. In 2011-2012, that figure has actually *fallen* to 43,919! Further, the actual graduation rate of people with a medical degree has only increased by an average of 0.3% -- *that's right, 0.3%* -- since 1982-1983. How is the current system expected to react by the introduction of up to 30 million new members in a matter of years when the number of qualified physicians is increasing by just 0.3% annually?

My suspicion is that patient care will be negatively affected, and those wanting covered but non-necessary exams as deemed by physicians, will be waiting even longer for the care they desire."

I suggest that adding a feature that is NOT part of the Canadian healthcare system can easily solve this problem. In Canada, there is no charge at all for routine visits to general practitioners. This encourages lonely and isolated people and others who are afflicted with minor illnesses or injuries that could be easily dealt with by over-the counter remedies, to make frivolous appointments with their physicians.

Therefore:

6. I believe a $20 charge should be levied on any person who visits a physician more than twice in any thirty-day period for routine treatment of the *same*

malady. **Each practitioner would be entitled to waive this fee if he or she feels a waiver is warranted.**

(The other 3 issues raised by Mr. Williams pertain to private insurance companies and the premiums Americans and/or their employers would be forced to pay. I have already addressed these topics.)

As I just explained, I believe that charging a small fee for excessive visits to a general practitioner will alleviate most of Mr. Williams' concerns about overloading doctors. In addition, I don't think that he's taken into account the growing practice of using **Physician Assistants (PAs)** to deliver healthcare services, which I discussed earlier in this chapter.

There is another deficiency in the Canadian healthcare system that I believe should be avoided if my framework is adopted in the U.S. *In Canada, the same provincial health care premium applies whether one is a smoker or non-smoker.*

Therefore:

7. I recommend that cigarette smokers be required to pay higher costs for health care than non-smokers.

There is likely to be less of an outcry with respect to this proposal than one might think. Today, insurance companies already charge cigarette smokers higher premiums for health (and life) insurance. If, under the system I am recommending, a smoker's costs were significantly lower than he or she currently pays, there is not likely to be much resistance to a two-tired system.

Enforcement is not really an issue. Under a federal or state administered program, everyone would presumably receive a colored plastic picture identification card encoded with his or her relevant data. This card would allow every service provider to bill the system for services rendered. Smokers could easily be issued a different colored card from non-smokers.

If one wanted to buy cigarettes, he or she should be required to present a smoker's healthcare card. In the same way that it is illegal today for a minor to purchase alcohol or tobacco products or for someone to buy these products for consumption by a minor, it would become illegal to buy tobacco products that are not for one's personal use. In addition, if someone with a non-smoker's card seeks professional care, and the medical practitioner has reason to believe that the patient is actually a smoker, the practitioner would be required to communicate his or her findings to the authorities. Fines could be levied and/or care costs could be charged back to the patient.

This is not as harsh a rule as you might think. Current industry practice allows a life insurance company to deny a claim if the claimant has lied about his or her use of tobacco.

8. I recommend that pharmaceutical companies be restricted from advertising drugs in media markets directed towards consumers and that prescription prices be regulated by the government.

I believe it is incumbent on the medical profession to recommend medications to patients and not the other way around. Often, a T.V. advertisement doesn't even mention the ailment it is designed to treat!

Eliminating media advertising would serve to reduce manufacturers' costs and the savings would hopefully be passed on.

In Canada, the government has negotiated prescription drug agreements with manufacturers and pharmacies to regulate prices that can be charged to consumers. I recommend that this be done in the U.S. as well.

9. I suggest that medical practitioners should be permitted to advertise their services, as is the case today.

Although I can see no valid reason to restrict physicians from advertising, I believe most doctors will be quite busy as many uninsured persons become insured under a state or federal program. Specialists in fields like cosmetic surgery would probably continue to advertise services not covered by the healthcare program.

10. Fee structures designed by the government to cover healthcare should be designed to provide *privately owned hospitals* the opportunity to earn reasonable returns on invested capital.

These fee structures should take into account that hospitals would benefit from a large reduction in their malpractice insurance premiums, if the malpractice awards structure were generally capped at reasonable amounts, as I suggested earlier in this chapter.

11. I recommend that fitness center memberships become a covered expenditure under a revamped socialized healthcare program, as long as certain conditions are met.

I believe preventative measures should be built into the healthcare system to ensure that many more people assume responsibility for their own well-being. Our obesity statistics are abysmal. **Statistically, the United States ranks as the second most overweight country in the world behind Mexico.**

I therefore recommend that Americans be encouraged to join low-cost fitness centers that agree to participate in a subsidized program along the following lines:
1. The maximum monthly membership that the healthcare system would cover should be set at (around) $50 per person.
2. Individual members would pay these fees personally.
3. To qualify for government reimbursement, the individual would be required to use the facility's fitness equipment, machines and weights for at least 20 hours per month. Facility staff would keep sign in/sign out cards for each member.
4. If the above conditions were met, the individual would be permitted to request an attendance certificate at six-month intervals. (Maximum $300 for a six-month period).
5. On filing a tax return, the individual would then claim

a credit in computing taxes payable or refundable. The maximum credit would be $600 a year.

I believe it is highly unlikely that high-income taxpayers will join low-cost fitness centers. If there is concern that a few wealthy people might try to beat the system, rules could be implemented to exclude the tax credit if adjusted gross income exceeds a certain level. Personally, I really don't believe this is really necessary.

12. I recommend that Medicare for seniors be abolished, subject to certain special provisions.

Shocked you, didn't I? I've saved the best for last! Here's my reasoning:

If everyone is covered by a nation-wide healthcare system, there is really no need for a special program for seniors. Low-income seniors would be exempted from paying monthly health care charges-the same as anyone else in that position.

For most seniors, monthly costs for socialized healthcare would be substantially less than they are paying now for supplementary insurance and co-pays. There are, however, some special program benefits that I recommend for seniors.

I believe that the healthcare system should cover the following costs for seniors:
1. 50% of routine dental work (not covered by the general healthcare system) up to $2,000 per annum.
2. Hearing aid costs of up to $3,500 every two years.

3. A daily subsidy for *basic* nursing home care that takes into account one's ability to pay.
4. 50% of prescription costs

13. Funding for a nation-wide health care system.

Clearly, I couldn't possibly be in a position to estimate the cost of establishing a nation-wide healthcare system. All I can suggest is that, if many other countries can afford to fund theirs, so can the United States. For a long time now, Americans have paid a 1.45% tax on their entire annual salaries and wages to fund Medicare for seniors. Their employers have matched this tax. Self-employed persons have been paying 2.9% (i.e. double).

Transforming this tax into healthcare premiums would go a long way towards providing funding. In addition, tax dollars that have been collected over the years but not yet spent on senior healthcare could be funneled into the new program. This is because, as I mentioned above, seniors would continue to pay the *same monthly health care levies as everyone else, although they would be entitled to some additional benefits.*

Let's make our healthcare system work! Mr. Obama, please read this.

Question 58: **Do you agree that Obamacare should be repealed?**

Yes___ No___ Undecided___

Question 59: **Do you agree that adopting a system of socialized medicine does not equate to embracing Communism?**

Yes___ No___ undecided___

Question 60: **Do you agree that concerns about potential patient satisfaction should be deferred until actual results are in- no matter what healthcare system is adopted?**

Yes___ No___ Undecided

Question 61: **Do you agree that a cost- effective healthcare system cannot exist if profit-oriented insurance companies administer it?**

Yes___ No___ Undecided___

Question 62: **Do you agree that, for a healthcare system to be effective, malpractice claims and awards should be regulated to protect physicians and reduce costs that are passed on to patients?**

Yes___ No___ Undecided___

Question 63: **Do you agree that a healthcare system should not erode our employment base by encouraging employers to outsource work and/or hire part-timers?**

Yes___ No___ Undecided___

Question 64: **Do you agree that,** *IF a socialized healthcare program is adopted* **a nominal charge ($20) would be appropriate in cases where a person visits a physician more than twice in a thirty-day period for routine treatment of the same malady?**

Yes___ No___ Undecided___

Question 65: **Please answer ONLY IF YOU ARE A NON-SMOKER.**
Do you agree that smokers should pay higher costs than non-smokers if socialized healthcare is adopted?

Yes___ No___ Undecided___

Question 66: **Please answer ONLY IF YOU ARE A SMOKER.**
Do you agree that smokers should pay higher costs than non-smokers if socialized healthcare is adopted?

Yes___ No___ Undecided___

Question 67: **Do you agree that pharmaceutical companies should not direct advertising towards consumers?**

Yes___ No___ Undecided___

Question 68: **Do you agree that, if a socialized healthcare system is adopted, the government should regulate prescription prices?**

Yes___ No__ Undecided___

Question 69: **Do you agree that, if a socialized healthcare system is adopted, the government should negotiate fees charged by *privately owned* hospitals so that they may earn a reasonable rate of return on invested capital?**

Yes___ No___ Undecided___

Question70: **Do you agree that, if a socialized healthcare system is adopted, reasonable fitness center membership fees should be included as part of the coverage program, subject to reasonable minimum usage requirements?**

Yes___ No___ Undecided___

Question 71: **Do you agree that, if a socialized healthcare system is adopted, seniors should be included in the overall program as long as their costs are less than average amounts paid under the current system?**

Yes___ No___ Undecided___

Do you agree that, if a socialized healthcare system is adopted, seniors should receive the following benefits that they do not currently receive?

Question 72: **50% of routine dental work (not covered by the general healthcare system) up to $2,000 per annum.**

Question 73: **Hearing aid costs of up to $3,500 every two years.**

Question 74: **A daily subsidy for *basic* nursing home care that takes into account one's ability to pay.**

Question 75: **50% of prescription costs?**

Question 72   Yes___ No___ Undecided___

Question 73   Yes___ No___ Undecided___

Question 74   Yes___ No___ Undecided___

Question 75   Yes___ No___ Undecided___

CHAPTER 8
REFORMING THE U.S. TAX SYSTEM

On July 25, 2013, I came across an article on MarketWatch.com stating that the U.S. Senate was soliciting ideas for what deductions and credits to keep as part of a study on tax reform. **The Senate Finance Committee promised that all submissions would be kept secret for 50 years**. So much for transparency within our government!

Many years ago, I was asked by a world-renowned ophthalmologist to sit on the board of directors of a foundation he had set up for ocular research. I agreed and attended two meetings before I resigned. I simply didn't have the knowledge or training to understand the issues and to contribute in a meaningful way.

Well, after over 40 years of immersion inside the wonderful world of taxation, I believe I do understand most of the ins and outs of the system. Some of my recommendations in this chapter are geared towards building a more equitable framework that meshes with my ideas on Enlightened Capitalism. Others are geared merely towards the goal of tax simplification.

Do you think the members of the Senate Finance Committee will read this chapter?

In each instance, I will explain the problem and what I suggest can be done to fix it. In most cases, I will try to keep the presentation simple, although certain issues may be difficult to grasp if your exposure to U.S. taxation is limited. As always, I encourage you to vote on my suggestions. If you feel that you are not able to formulate a decisive opinion, please use the "undecided" option.

1. **I believe estate taxes and gift taxes should be abolished.**

I thought I'd start out with a biggy! I am not making this recommendation because I am in the pocket of the mega-wealthy. Rather, I believe that the existing capital gains legislation can be expanded very easily to make estate and gift taxes r*edundant*.

First, here is some background. Before 1972, Canada had a very simple tax structure. Capital gains were *totally tax-free*. In that year, the Canadian tax system underwent a major reform. Most of the Canadian tax changes were either copied from, or were modifications of, rules in the U.S. Internal Revenue Code.

A simple example is the rule that now applies in both countries providing that only 50% of business meals and entertainment costs qualify as an allowable deduction for tax purposes.

One major difference, however, was that, when

the Canadian government introduced its proposals to tax capital gains, they were able *to eliminate the country's previous estate and gift tax laws.*

Here's the reasoning. **It is based on the premise that every dollar you have in your jeans represents after-tax income.** (Even if you earn a very low income, it would theoretically be taxable if there weren't other rules that erase your potential liability through deductions and credits.)

Once income is taxed, it is really unfair to tax that same income a second time. The current tax system in the U.S. first taxes the wealthy when they make capital gains. Then, although there is a liberal estate tax exemption, **in many cases at least part of** *the same original gain is taxed a second time when the person dies.*

I know that many Americans have little sympathy for the very wealthy. **However, my version of Enlightened Capitalism is not intended to bankrupt anyone. In most cases, affluent people will still be our economic leaders. All I want, is to strive for fairness and the wealthy, like the rest of us, require reasonable incentives to take risk and/or produce goods and services.**

Here is an example that illustrates the double-taxation issue that I have raised. (It ignores the fact that estate tax in the U.S. can be deferred-but not eliminated- if property is bequeathed to a spouse.)

Assume a wealthy individual makes a $1 Million investment that is eventually sold for $11 Million several years later

Long-term capital gain	$10 Million
Tax in highest bracket (20%)*	2 Million
After-tax income	$8 Million

========

When the individual dies:
Amount of after -tax income included in estate

$8 Million

Assumed lifetime estate tax exemption

$5 Million (Actually $5,250,000)

| Amount subject to estate tax | $3 Million |

========

| Tax at maximum rate of 40% (2013) | $1.2 Million |

========

*Maximum tax on long-term capital gains in 2013

In the above example, the total tax on the original gain of $10 million becomes $3.2 million, or 32%- not much less than the top tax rate of 39.6% on ordinary income.

I hope you can understand that the concept of an estate tax is unfair. Note that, under current U.S. tax law, large gifts made in one's lifetime are added back and included in the base for estate taxes. Since cash gifts represent income that was previously taxed, the concept that an estate tax is unfair extends to a gift tax as well.

Of course, you might ask the question, if gift and estate taxes were eliminated, what would stop anyone from holding on to property that has appreciated in value until death or gifting it in his or her lifetime to children or grandchildren to avoid paying taxes on the accumulated capital gains?

The Canadian authorities solved that potential problem by incorporating the concept of **"deemed dispositions"** directly into their capital gains legislation.

In Canada, **if one dies holding capital property (including real estate), it is deemed to have been sold at fair market value in the instant before death** (unless the property is "rolled over" to a spouse, in which case, the deemed disposition is deferred until the second spouse's death, if it is not sold before then).

The deemed disposition triggers capital gains or losses that are reported on the deceased person's final tax return

There are special rules that allow family farms to be passed on without taxation to children or grandchildren, as well as a special rule that exempts up to $750,000 of capital gains (during one's lifetime or on death) arising with respect to Canadian-owned small business corporation shares. I believe similar exemptions should apply in the United States if the estate tax is repealed and the capital gains legislation is extended.

In Canada, if one makes a gift of capital property (including real estate) to anyone other than a spouse, this also triggers a deemed disposition at market value and the gain, if any, is reported on the transferor's tax return for that year. Capital losses on transfers of property to close relatives are not permitted, as is the case already in the U.S.

To summarize, I recommend that U.S. estate and gift taxes be repealed and replaced with deemed disposition rules to
1. **trigger capital gains at the time growth property is gifted to anyone other than a spouse,**
2. **trigger a deemed sale at market value of growth property at the time of death, unless property is left to a spouse (or a trust where the spouse receives all the income as long as (s)he lives).**

In all cases of *non-spousal* transfers, the recipient's cost for tax purposes would become an amount equal to the transferor's deemed proceeds. This would prevent the same gain from being taxed twice.

In fact, if the deemed disposition concept were adopted, total U.S. tax revenues would actually *increase*. This is because these rules would apply to *everyone* who owns growth property (other than a primary residence, or a small businesses/family farm, where exemptions would apply). Under the present estate tax rules there is a total exemption for estates worth less than $5,250,000. *This exemption would be scrapped automatically if all the Estate Tax and Gift Tax provisions were eliminated.*

For example, if one had a stock portfolio with a tax cost of $100,000 and it was worth $300,000 when the person died, a $200,000 gain would be reportable on

the final tax return (unless the portfolio is bequeathed to a spouse.) The heirs would assume a $300,000 cost for tax purposes since their inheritance would come to them in the form of tax-paid assets. Some part of the portfolio may have to be sold to pay the tax on the deemed capital gain. The deemed disposition concept actually lifts some of the tax burden from the shoulders of the very wealthy. I believe this is a good example of social responsibility being a two-way street.

In 1996, two university professors, Thomas J. Stanley and William D. Danko, wrote a best-selling book called "The Millionaire Next Door". By surveying high-income postal codes, they were able to characterize the "typical" American millionaire.

Perhaps surprisingly, the profile that they compiled was not that of the high-flying financial wizard or tech guru. *It was the second or third generation mid-western business owner who lived frugally and spent wisely.*

What is interesting is that the authors postulated that the special millionaire characteristics of drive, thriftiness etc. were not being passed on by the parents to their children. In an effort to reduce potential estate taxes, millionaires generally took advantage of the fact that it was acceptable to make annual tax-free gifts to any person of up to (at that time) $10,000 a year.

Thus, if wealthy parents had a recently-married son or daughter, they could *each* give $10,000 to *both* their child and his or her spouse. According to Professors Stanley and Danko, $40,000 a year of tax-free support often eliminated any incentive for the children to succeed on their own. At the present time, the annual allowance for tax-free gifts is $14,000 a year.

Eliminating estate taxes would remove the incentive of gift-giving simply to "beat" the system. This is another example of social responsibility.

2. Pension plans should be abolished and replaced with Individual Retirement Accounts

This is another of my major recommended changes. I presented my "arguments" in Chapter 5. In order to keep all my tax reform proposals in one place, I will simply repeat my recommendations here without reiterating all my reasons. *I will not put this matter to a vote at the end of this chapter because these proposals are on the "ballot" for Chapter 5.*

If pension plans are to be terminated, I recommend that the assets should be allocated fairly among the different classes of participants in the following order:

i. Former employees who have already retired
ii. Employees age 55-65 who are willing to take early retirement
iii. Employees age 55-65 who will be retaining their employment
iv. Employees age 45-55
v. Employees age 35-45
vi. Employees under age 35

Each group would be required to share to some extent in any shortfall, with younger employees assuming the major portion of the total deficiency since, as a group, they have more time to recoup their losses.

I also recommend that each beneficiary's distribution should flow without any current taxation into a personal IRA. Each person would generally be prohibited from making withdrawals until age 59 ½, as is now the case. Employers should be required to provide and pay for up to two hours of investment consulting advice through independent firms so that employees could tailor their plans to suit their individual circumstances.

In addition, I believe that a realistic formula to expand IRA limits should be introduced that would be indexed from time-to-time:

A. There should be a mandatory annual employer contribution to each employee's IRA of 8% of salaries and wages to an annual maximum of $10,000 (8% x $125,000). *

B. Each employee should be permitted to match the employer's contribution in *whole or in part,* generally by way of deductions withheld from paychecks. The employee's contribution could be made into either a regular IRA or a Roth IRA ** at the employee's request

C. Employee contributions to a regular IRA

should be tax deductible. *In addition, all of the employee's contributions should qualify for a 25% tax credit.* (The deduction would essentially refund 25% of the average employee's contribution, assuming an average Federal tax bracket of 25%, and the 25% tax credit would reduce his or her cost to only half of the contribution.)

D. The "use it or lose it" tax rules should be repealed. Any eligible amount not contributed by an employee in a given year should be available for an unlimited carry forward to any subsequent year. This provision would take into account the fact that a family's ability to save increases once their home is paid and there are no longer dependent children at home.

3. The maximum federal tax on earned income should be 33.3%

In Chapter 3, I proposed a maximum tax rate of 33.3% on earned income. I don't believe that it is really necessary to impose higher taxes on the non-investment-related earnings of those relatively few people. (*I also made this one of my poll questions*). I will briefly repeat my suggestions on limiting executive remuneration even though these do not necessarily require amendments to the Internal Revenue Code.

The maximum executive remuneration of any individual (whether by salary, benefits, stock options, or any other means of compensation) employed by a U.S. company should *initially* be set at a base of $1.5 Million dollars. The maximum tax rate on earned

income of up to $1.5 Million should be set at 33.3%. These rules should apply to all companies with 5 or more employees whether public or private.

Once this level of remuneration is reached, additional compensation could then be paid <u>provided</u> *each employee who has been with the employer for at least 2 years receives a bonus of at least 5% of the average additional remuneration paid out to all executives within the employer company who will earn in excess of $1.5 Million that year.* The 5% bonuses would become part of the employees' base pay for the subsequent and succeeding years.

In the event that any executive's income exceeds $1.5 million because of stock option benefits that could not be estimated or quantified in advance and the required bonuses to the other employees are not paid, the executive would be required to *refund the excess* to the company.

Retirement payments and "golden parachute" payments to executives whose employment has been terminated because of a buy-out should be limited to three times average remuneration for the previous three years.

For purposes of these rules, if a group of related companies exists, all remuneration paid to any one person would be added together to avoid circumventing the income limits. Companies and their executives will be prohibited from avoiding these rules through the payment of consulting fees.

4. I recommend that the Internal Revenue Code be amended to simply exclude the first $1 Million of *lifetime gains* (or deemed gains) *of any individual* with respect to sales or transfers of small active-business corporations and family farms, as long as these have been held for 5 years or longer. (This would replace the far more complex provisions under present law.) If spouses owned a qualified business or farm jointly, the total exemption should become $2 Million.

Since this is merely a simplification of existing provisions, I believe no further explanation is necessary

5. I recommend setting a small business corporate tax rate of 20% on the first $250,000 of *annual active business earnings* of private corporations, as long as the after-tax profits are reinvested for business growth.

Under current tax law, only the first $75,000 of corporate business profits is taxed at low rates of between 15% and 25%. The low rate benefits are phased out gradually if these profits exceed $100,000. Increasing the low rate base will encourage *privately owned* small businesses to grow. To qualify, the after-tax income would have to be employed to expand the business and not to make passive investments on behalf of the owners. There is already a set of rules in the Internal Revenue Code that allows the I.R.S. to impose a 15% "Accumulated Earnings Tax" that applies on excessive retained earnings over $250,000 that are not used for business expansion.

As is the case today, if a business earns income from services, my suggested tax benefits would only apply if the corporation is truly carrying on an active business and is not being used to mask or tax-shelter employment income.

(As an aside, Canada's small businesses pay low tax rates on up to $500,000 each year and there is no requirement that after-tax profits be deployed towards business expansion. I believe this is overly generous.)

6. I recommend that the general corporate tax rate on active business income that does not qualify for the small business tax rate be set at 30%

In Chapter 3, I recommended that foreign earnings of American large businesses be subjected to U.S. taxation whether or not they are repatriated. If this is legislated, the base for U.S. corporate taxes will expand significantly. I believe that the tax rate should be adjusted downward accordingly to give American companies added incentive to create domestic jobs.

7. I recommend that the Subchapter S Corporation rules be repealed as long as corporate tax rates are reduced in accordance with my last two recommendations

The concept of Subchapter S Corporations was originally introduced to allow *privately owned businesses* to take advantage of limited liability for shareholders, while avoiding the pitfall of high taxes on corporate business income coupled with taxes on dividend distributions (that until a few years ago were taxed as ordinary income). A Subchapter S Corporation is treated as a proprietorship or partnership and its income flows through to the "owner(s)" without corporate tax. Only personal tax rates apply.

Over the past few years, several changes have occurred. First, the concept of limited liability partnerships has been embraced by many organizations to provide the same protection as S Corporations. Secondly, the tax on corporate dividend distributions is now generally only 15%. This substantially reduces the impact of double taxation. Finally, **if** the small business tax rate is adjusted to 20% on the first $250,000 of business income, 80 cents on the dollar (80%) becomes potentially distributable to individual shareholders. If the tax on dividends is 15% of the 80%, the retention factor will be 85% x 80% or 68%. The *total* tax bite becomes a *more or less* acceptable 32%. (Please see my next recommendation.) This would make S Corporations obsolete.

8. I agree with *part of* President Obama's recent legislation that sets the tax rate on dividend income received by individuals in the highest tax bracket at 20% (taxable income in excess of $400,000-$450,000, depending on filing status). However, **I recommend that dividends paid by *private* companies should only be subjected to a 10% tax in the hands of any individual recipient.** I believe that the 20% tax should only apply to dividends from investments in ***publicly traded companies.***

If my recommended change were made, all individuals would retain 90% of private company dividends, or 72 cents out of each dollar instead of 68%.

Assumed business earnings	$100
Assumed corporate tax (20%)	20
After tax profit paid as a dividend	80
Personal tax on dividend (10%)	8
After-tax retention by individual	$72

====

9. I strongly suggest that the system of recording depreciation for income tax purposes be simplified by reducing the number of asset categories and by adopting a single method for depreciation calculations.

I believe that an efficient, yet simple, tax depreciation system for business property can be structured if all such assets are allocated to one of four classes:

Annual Rate of Depreciation
Class1. Buildings other than wood-frame buildings*

(2.5%)

Class 2. Wood-frame buildings* (4.0%)

Class 3. Automobiles, trucks, machinery, computers and peripherals, (20.0%)

Class 4. Office furniture and fixtures and anything not included above (10.0%)

* Each building owned should be allocated to a separate "Class 1" or "Class 2" so that gains or losses could be accurately computed at the time of sale.

In the year of acquisition, one-half of a full year's depreciation should be allowed. There should be no allowable depreciation in the year of disposition.

Depreciation should be calculated on a declining balance basis. This method results in higher depreciation allowances in the earlier years. The theory is that repairs and maintenance increase as property ages. If depreciation and maintenance are considered together, the cost of ownership is amortized more or less equally over time.

Here is an example of declining balance depreciation:

Office furniture acquired in year 1	$10,000
Depreciation year 1 10% x $10,000 X ½*	$500
Undepreciated cost	$ 9,500
Depreciation year 2 10% x $9,500	$950
Undepreciated cost	$ 8,550
Depreciation year 3 10% x $8,550	$ 855
Undepreciated cost	$ 7,695

*One-half of "normal" depreciation applies in the year of acquisition.

From time to time, it may be expedient to offer tax incentives for acquisitions of depreciable property by way of allowing costs to be expensed in full in the year of purchase. The mechanics already exist (Section 179) and I would retain this provision.

10. Opportunities to transfer property to a corporation without triggering immediate taxes should be made more flexible.

Under the current tax rules, property can only be "rolled over" without tax to a corporation if the transferor (or transferors) own(s) at least 80% of the shares of the recipient company. This is very restrictive.

In 1972, when Canada introduced taxes on capital gains and "borrowed" many of its rules from the U.S. Internal Revenue Code, they too limited the tax-free transfer rules to incorporate the 80% requirement. In 1973, Canada withdrew this requirement and I'm not aware of any adverse repercussions over the last 40 years.

Also, the U.S. tax rules only permit the transferor to receive *shares* on a tax-free basis. If any other consideration is received, the rollover is partially negated. This is unfair. **One should be able to recover his or her cost without adverse consequences. This is because, as I explained earlier, one can only acquire property in the first place with dollars on which taxes have already been paid.**

The Canadian rules permit cost-recovery and, again I've not heard of any complaints about lost tax revenues in the past 40 years. The rules are structured so that the transferor must receive sufficient share value so that no retroactive gifts of accumulated growth are made to related parties.

11. In Chapter 4, I proposed a 10% surtax on net day trading profits of all *financial institutions (both publicly and privately owned).*

Earlier, I explained my reasoning for this proposal. I am simply repeating it here to keep all my tax suggestions together. Question 37 allows you to vote on this issue.

12. The state and municipal tax-free bond rules require amendment to incorporate tax-free reciprocity between all the states

For many years, The U.S. Tax Code has permitted Americans to earn tax-free interest from state and municipal bonds in order to allow these entities to raise borrowed capital at lower rates than would otherwise apply. Each state has rules under which interest from bond issues *from within that state* are also tax-free when filing that particular state's tax return. However, interest on *another* state's debt **is** taxable in the state of residence. For example, a resident of Virginia pays no tax on a Virginia municipality's bond interest, while interest from a Pennsylvania bond would be taxable.

The accounting becomes very complex in cases where an individual owns bond funds. The proportion of "home state" interest can vary frequently over the course of any given year, as fund managers buy and sell different securities, and there are additional complications where bond fund units are bought or sold by the particular individual periodically during a given year.

From personal experience, I can attest to the fact that tax preparation fees resulting from bond fund ownership can outstrip the tax savings from any tax-free interest.

I therefore recommend that a reciprocity arrangement be brokered by the federal government to make all of this interest tax free on any state income tax return, no matter which (other state) is the source of the income.

13. I believe that the alternative minimum tax provisions in the Internal Revenue Code should be eliminated.

The alternative minimum tax (AMT) was first introduced over 30 years ago to ensure that everyone, whether individual or corporation, pays at least some taxes and cannot unreasonably avoid paying a "fair share". The AMT provisions are complex and cumbersome. Certain write-offs and deductions that are claimed to reduce regular tax otherwise payable are added back in arriving at taxable income subject to this tax.

There are several problems with the AMT. The first is that many middle-income taxpayers must prepare the voluminous paperwork necessary to prove that they are not subject to this tax. Secondly, as I pointed out in Chapter 3, only 5% of taxpayers have adjusted gross incomes in excess of about $160,000.

Few people are actually affected by the AMT. The most common situation where the alternative minimum tax would apply is where a taxpayer claims oil and gas, mining, or research and development write-offs. Frankly, if taxpayers are making these investments, they are creating jobs.

There are "regular" tax provisions in the Tax Code that govern the tax treatment these expenditures. To me, it makes little sense for the income tax structure to give with one hand and take back with the other.

14. To encourage responsible borrowing and fairness, I recommended the following provisions in Chapter 6:

1. **The Internal Revenue Code should be amended to restrict the deductibility of home mortgage interest (and property taxes) to costs incurred with respect to ONE primary residence.**

2. **The maximum debt that qualifies for deductibility of interest should be limited to THREE TIMES the adjusted gross income of the person or persons (in case a joint return is filed) who are claiming the deduction.**

3. **The overall qualifying home mortgage debt limit on which interest is tax-deductible should be reduced from $1 Million to $500,000.**

I also recommended two further changes.

4. **While interest on credit card debt and (personal-use) automobile loans is not deductible, there is a tax provision whereby homeowners can deduct interest on up to $100,000 of "Home Equity Lines of Credit' (HELOCS). In order to foster responsible borrowing, I recommend that the deductibility of such interest be restricted to situations where the loan proceeds are used for *structural home additions and improvements*. Prospective borrowers would be required to present project proposals to lenders, along with**

quotations from contactors and suppliers, before financing could be secured. In addition, upon completion, copies of invoices from the trades would be required for lenders' files.

To qualify for home mortgage interest deductibility, mortgage terms should be limited to *fifteen years*. If a home mortgage is refinanced, to retain deductibility, the maximum term of the refinancing should be limited to fifteen years minus the term that has elapsed since the initial mortgage financing was granted

In Chapter 6, I explained my reasoning for these proposals and, again, I am simply repeating them here to keep all my tax recommendations together. The questions following Chapter 6 are designed to let you vote on these matters.

15. I recommend that the deduction for interest on money borrowed for investment purpose be taken into account in determining adjusted gross income and not treated as an itemized deduction.

My reasoning is that this interest on money borrowed for investments **pertains directly** to the income-earning process. I have no quarrel with the rule that restricts the deduction to do no more than offset the amount of investment income earned in a given year, subject to the carryover of excess interest expense against investment income of future years. I think most people who itemize deductions claim home mortgage interest. Someone who either rents *or has paid off a home* may not have sufficient total itemized deductions to take reasonable advantage of investment interest paid, unless the deduction becomes part of the adjusted gross income calculation.

16. I recommend that the deduction for outside salesman expenses and unreimbursed employee expenses, including job training *and retraining,* be taken into account in determining adjusted gross income and not as an itemized deduction.

My reasoning is the same as my reasoning with respect to investment interest expense. These costs relate directly to the income earning process and anyone who incurs such expenses should be allowed to claim them.

17. I recommend that the deduction for job training expenses be expanded to include job-*retraining* costs that would lead to potential *new* jobs.

I am amazed that the federal government needs to be told to expand this deduction. The present rules only allow a deduction for training costs incurred with respect to one's *current* job. Many "old" jobs are obsolete-especially as a result of outsourcing and technology.

People who invest in themselves and are willing to make changes and sacrifices should be rewarded, not punished. I'm sure the I.R.S. can recognize courses that are really geared towards personal hobbies and interests. Claims for these should obviously be disallowed.

18. The tax rules for "claw backs" of deductions and credits otherwise available to higher income persons should be standardized in order to provide a common definition of what constitutes a "high-income person".

There are many deductions and credits that are taken away or reduced for high-income taxpayers. The rules were all introduced at different times and the income levels at which "claw backs", as they are often called, begin to apply are all different.

For example:

- In 2012, up to 50% of social security payments became taxable for married taxpayers if adjusted gross income + ½ of social security benefits + tax exempt income exceeded $32,000.

- The opportunity to deduct rental losses (where the taxpayer is actively involved in his or her rental activities) against other income is limited is $25,000. This deduction is phased out beginning when the taxpayer's adjusted gross income exceeds $100,000.

- The child tax credit begins its phase-out for married taxpayers with modified adjusted gross incomes of $110,000.

- Childcare credits are reduced if adjusted gross income exceeds $15,000.

- If one is a member of a pension plan, Individual Retirement Account (IRA) allowable contributions are phased out above certain income limits. The limits are not the same for regular IRAs and Roth IRAs.

If the authorities feel that claw backs are really necessary, let's standardize them.

19. The child and dependent care credits should be restructured to reflect "real life" costs. I believe there should be no phase-out for higher income families.

These credits are designed to assist individuals to seek or retain employment. *The advantage of a credit, compared to a deduction, is that anyone who is otherwise paying taxes is able to reduce the "bite" by the same amount, as long as their eligible costs are the same.*

I recommend that these credits should only be available in cases where a dependent is under age 14 or is incapacitated. I believe the credit should be 25% of expenditures of up to $10,000 for each of the first two dependents and expenditures of $5,000 for each additional dependent.

In the case of a married couple, I suggest that the maximum allowable costs on which the credit is based should not exceed 50% of the earned income of the lower-income spouse. If there is only one supporting individual, eligible costs should not exceed 50% of his or her earned income.

Here is an example in which a married couple employs a housekeeper primarily to look after their children:

Spouse X earned income	$50,000
Spouse Y earned income	$30,000
Number of children under 14	3
Total costs incurred for housekeeper	$32,000

Maximum costs to be considered	$25000
($10,000 + $10,000 + $5,000)	
Maximum costs based on Spouse Y's Earned income	
	$15,000
(50% x $30,000)	
Tax credit (25%)	$3,750

In this case, half of Spouse Y's income would be tax-free since the couple is in the 25% tax bracket.

You might ask why I am recommending that childcare costs be given tax credit treatment. After all, they are actually expenses incurred to earn income and it might be technically more appropriate to treat them as deductions in arriving at adjusted gross income.

Childcare costs, however, will often be the same, whether a family has a high income or a moderate income. If I am a single parent and I earn $100,000 a year, it might cost me $800 a month to send a young child to a local daycare. If you are a single parent and you earn $40,000, it would probably cost the same amount for you to send your young child the same daycare. *I believe both of us should get the same tax benefit.*

20. The deduction for tuition fees of up to $4,000, which is phased out for high-income taxpayers, should

be eliminated and replaced by a modified Lifetime Learning Credit of 25% on up to $10,000 of post-secondary tuition fees and related costs per student, per annum. Eligible educational institutions should include post-secondary vocational schools that award diplomas upon successful completion of studies.

The present $4,000 deduction limit for tuition fees and related costs is unrealistic and is unfair to higher income persons. (Please remember-the concept of social responsibility extends to everyone). As I mentioned above, *the advantage of a credit, compared to a deduction, is that anyone who is otherwise paying taxes is able to reduce their bite by the same amount, as long as their eligible costs are the same.*

At the present time, the Lifetime Learning Credit is 20% on up to $10,000 of qualified costs. I would raise the credit to 25%. Thus, anyone who spends $10,000 would recover $2,500, as long as his or her tax bill before the claim is at least that amount.

If this proposal is adopted, a deduction for actual fees becomes redundant, as does the Hope Scholarship Credit, which covers up to the first two years of post-secondary tuition costs.

I believe the United States should be putting more emphasis on vocational training and less emphasis on traditional universities. As such, I recommend that the rules for the Lifetime Learning Credit should be extended to apply to vocational schools that grant diplomas (and not degrees).

21. The deduction for interest on educational loans of up to $2,500 per annum, which is phased out for high income taxpayers, should be replaced by a 25% credit on up to $4,000 of interest annually.

Again, I believe that phased-out deductions are cumbersome and unfair. A 25% credit based on an interest limit of up to $4,000 would reduce the tax of all qualified claimants by as much as $1,000 a year as long as they have taxable incomes before this credit. If one assumes an interest rate of 4% and the fact that final college and university debt often tops $100,000, a $4,000 base becomes more realistic than $2,500.

22. Tax-deductible contributions to Coverdell Education Savings Accounts (also referred to as Education IRAs), that are currently phased out for high-income persons, should be replaced by a 25% tax credit on contributions of up to $4,000 a year *with no phase-out*. I recommend that the credit should only apply to savings for post-secondary education.

The current limit considered for tax purposes for annual Education IRAs is $2,000. I believe $4,000 is more realistic. $4,000 a year earning 4% will amount to almost $102,600
over an 18-year period, from a child's birth until he or she usually completes high school.

It is, of course, impossible to project the costs of higher education that many years into the future. However, assuming grants and scholarships continue to be available, a six-figure savings account should go a long way towards reducing any student's eventual debt load at the end of his or her studies. The tax credit would provide all contributors with a potential $1,000 reduction in taxes each year.

The current rules allow these plans to be used to help fund private school education. I believe that, in the interest of fairness, they should only be used to fund post-secondary education. An exception should be made with respect to special needs situations.

23. Under current tax legislation personal exemptions are phased out for higher tax-bracket individuals. I believe the deduction should be replaced by a 25% tax credit so that all Americans would be treated equally. Eliminating the phase-out formulas would simplify the tax system as well.

Question 76: **Do you agree that estate and gift taxes should be repealed and replaced with deemed disposition rules to:**
   1. **trigger capital gains at the time growth property is gifted to anyone other than a spouse,**
   2. **trigger a deemed sale at market value of growth property at the time of death, unless property is left to a spouse (or a trust where the spouse receives all the income as long as (s)he lives)?**
(In all cases of *non-spousal* transfers, the recipient's cost for tax purposes would become an amount equal to the deemed proceeds to prevent the same gain from being taxed twice.)

Yes___ No___ Undecided___

Question 77: **Do you agree that the maximum federal tax on earned income should be 33.3%?**

Yes___ No___ Undecided___

Question 78: **Do you agree that that the Internal Revenue Code should be amended to simply exclude the first $1 Million of *lifetime gains* (or deemed gains) *of any individual* with respect to sales or transfers of small active-business corporations and family farms, as long as these have been held for 5 years or longer? (This would replace the far more complex provisions under present law.) If spouses owned a qualified business or farm jointly, the total exemption would become $2 Million.**

Yes___ No___ Undecided___

Question 79: **Do you agree that a small business corporate tax rate of 20% should apply to the first $250,000 of *annual active business earnings* of private corporations, as long as the after-tax profits are reinvested for business growth?**

Yes___ No___ Undecided___

Question 80: **Do you agree that the general corporate tax rate on active business income that does not qualify for the small business tax rate should be set at 30%?**

Yes___ No___ Undecided___

Question 81: **Do you agree that the Subchapter S Corporation rules should be repealed as long as the corporate tax rates are reduced in accordance with the last two recommendations?**

Yes___No___ Undecided___

Question 82: **Do you agree that dividends paid by private companies should only be subjected to a 10% tax in the hands of any individual recipient?**

Yes___ No___ Undecided___

Question 83: **Do you agree that the system of recording depreciation for income tax purposes should be simplified by reducing the number of asset categories and by adopting a single method for calculations?**

Yes___ No___ Undecided___

Question 84: **Do you agree that the rule requiring at least 80% ownership in order to transfer property without tax to a corporation should be repealed and that the transferor should be allowed to recover his or her cost of the property without tax?**

Yes___ No___ Undecided___

Question 85: **Do you agree that the state and municipal tax-free bond rules should be amended to incorporate tax-free reciprocity between all the states?**

Yes___ No___ Undecided___

Question 86: **Do you agree that the alternative minimum tax provisions should be eliminated completely?**

Yes___ No___ Undecided___

Question 87: **Do you agree that the deduction for interest on money borrowed for investment purpose should be taken into account in determining adjusted gross income and not as an itemized deduction?**

Yes___ No___ Undecided___

Question 88: **Do you agree that the deduction for outside salesman expenses and unreimbursed employee expenses, including job training *and retraining,* should be taken into account in determining adjusted gross income and not as an itemized deduction?**

Yes___ No___ Undecided___

Question 89: **Do you agree that the deduction for job training expenses should be expanded to include job-*retraining* costs that would lead to potential *new* jobs?**

Yes___ No___ Undecided___

Question 90: **Do you agree that the tax rules for "claw backs" of deductions and credits otherwise available to higher income persons should be standardized in order to provide a common definition of what constitutes a "high –income person"**

Yes___ No___ Undecided___

Question 91: **Do you agree that the child and dependent care credits should be restructured to reflect "real life" costs and that there should be no phase-out for higher income families?**

Yes___ No___ Undecided___

Question 92: **Do you agree that the deduction for tuition fees of up to $4,000, which is phased out for high-income taxpayers, should be eliminated and replaced by a modified Lifetime Learning Credit of 25% on up to $10,000 per student per annum of post-secondary tuition fees and related costs?**

Yes___ No___ Undecided___

Question 93: **Do you agree that eligible educational institutions should include post-secondary vocational schools that award diplomas upon successful completion of studies?**

Yes___ No___ Undecided___

Question 94: **Do you agree that the deduction for interest on educational loans of up to $2,500 per annum, which is phased out for high income taxpayers, should be replaced by a 25% credit on up to $4,000 of interest?**

Yes___ No___ Undecided___

Question 95: **Do you agree that tax-deductible contributions to Coverdell Education Savings Accounts (also referred to as Education IRAs) that are currently phased out for high-income persons, should be replaced by a 25% tax credit on contributions of up to $4,000 a year?**

Yes___ No___ Undecided___

Question 96: **Do you agree that the credit should only apply to savings for post-secondary education (or special needs education) and not to defray the costs of private or prep schools for younger children?**

Yes___ No___ Undecided___

Question 97: **Do you agree that the deduction for personal exemptions that is phased out for higher-income taxpayers should be replaced by a 25% tax credit so that all Americans will be treated equally?**

Yes___ No___ Undecided____

CHAPTER 9
REFORMING OUR NATION'S EDUCATIONAL SYSTEM

Many years ago, I had a crush on Kathleen Turner, a well-known actress. I've also loved the concept of time travel and, to this day, enjoy time travel novels especially when the characters interact with real historical figures. In 1986, the movie *"Peggy Sue Got Married"* was released starring Ms. Turner and Nicholas Cage. In this movie, a 30-something woman faints at a class reunion and wakes up as a high school senior with full memory recall. Going back to the classroom is a real pain for her, and, at one point, when asked why she didn't do her homework, she tells her math teacher, "I happen to know that in later life I won't have any use for algebra."

Perhaps you remember the Paul Simon song *"Kodachrome"*, which begins with the words "When I think back on all the crap I learned in high school, it's a wonder I can think at all."

Over the years, I've often thought about both the movie and the song. My highest marks in high school were

209

in trigonometry, algebra and chemistry. Today, I might use the most basic algebra to calculate stuff like: if 20% of x is 100, what is x? But that's it. I was good in history and English. I majored in English Lit at University and then went into accounting. As an undergraduate, I learned communication skills and, for that I am grateful.

The only mathematics I use now relates to financial planning- How much do I need to invest today to accumulate x in the future? If I have x today, and I draw y dollars a month, when will I run out of money? In my accountancy courses, I was forced to learn long-forgotten formulas. Today, we all have easy-to-use tables available at our fingertips on the Internet.

Unfortunately, I don't believe that many high schools today teach the minimal number crunching needed for every day living.

The goal of a traditional secondary school has been to provide a well-rounded education and to prepare students to enter colleges and universities. However, it is very much structured as a one-size-fits all mold. Yes, we all need to master the 3 "R's"- reading, 'riting and 'rithmetic. But do we *all* need to learn another language? Do we *all* need to learn chemistry or geometry?

Sure, there are classrooms allocated to students who don't excel in certain disciplines and they are designed to grind out a diploma at the end of the day. But what attempt is made to foster the individual aptitudes and interests of those students? How many drop out because of frustration?

When I was growing up in the years following World War II, young people were strongly encouraged to attend academic universities. Fortunately, it worked out for most of us. But that was before globalization, outsourcing and technology. Universities have always allowed students to pick and choose their areas of interest, subject to certain compulsory courses that were generally accepted as constituting an unavoidable part of a "means to an end".

Today, a large proportion of university undergraduates have no idea what they want to do after graduation. Even those who are focused on a career often have no idea what the job market will be like a few years down the road.

Recently, I struck up a conversation with a young lady at a dog park who told me that she has been substitute teaching for the last *eight* years while waiting for a full-time position. When she went off to college, she was told that California would need lots of teachers. But then came the cutbacks....

At the present time, I believe that anyone in America who has an aptitude in languages will have a "heads up" on most other people. There is already a very heavy demand for people fluent in English and Spanish. In my opinion, fluency in Cantonese should pay big dividends over the next twenty years.

My thesis in this chapter incorporates a strong recommendation that unbiased experts, who are willing to embrace change, must reexamine the objectives of our entire educational process. If we want to solve the

problem of youth unemployment, we must recognize that not everyone is suited to a traditional university education.

Recently, I came across an article that discussed how Germany deals with the issue of youth unemployment. There are two major components to their solution:

1. In their early teens, children are tested to determine their diverse aptitudes and interests. They are then streamlined into suitable programs *designed for them to succeed*.
2. Young people with the requisite interests and skill sets are placed into apprenticeships and work-study programs that provide "real life" experience.

This is what I will put to a vote at the end of this chapter: Should we in America be following the German model?

I believe we can learn from the German experience, as well as from the Scandinavian countries that seem to have solved the youth unemployment problem. We should try to apply the successes of other countries' experiences to our own youth problems.

Yes, there will be complaints. Parents with university degrees, for instance, may object to the placement of a son or daughter into a vocational training program. However, it is incumbent on parents to be realistic about their children's strengths and weaknesses. They should have the right to secure a second evaluation /opinion and may choose to send children to private schools if they wish.

When I graduated university in 1964, I began a three-year apprenticeship with an accounting firm at a starting salary of $40 a week. A modest apartment went for about $100 a month. In the end, it was all worth it!

For vocational students, a trade apprenticeship would lead to journeyman status and eventually to a master's license. Work-study programs and internships would also be an excellent method of integrating university students into the work force.

Earlier in this book, I recommended that the military take an active role in employing and training America's youth.

Most of what follows consists of excerpts from three articles that seem to confirm my thinking about the necessary changes that we need to make in the American educational system.

The first article is taken from business.time.com, a component of the online version of Time Magazine. It was written in November 2012 by Peter Gumbel.

Why the U.S. Has a Worse Youth Unemployment Problem than Europe

"The latest unemployment statistics released this week on both sides of the Atlantic show that the number of jobless is continuing to rise in Europe far above the rate in the U.S., and the picture is especially bleak for young Europeans under the age of 25. In the 27 E.U. nations as a whole, the youth unemployment rate rose to 22.8% in September, up from 21.7% the previous year. In Greece and Spain, that proportion is over 50%. In the U.S., meanwhile, the unemployment rate was essentially unchanged in October, at 7.9%, the Bureau of Labor Statistics announced Nov. 2. And the U.S. rate of unemployment among young people under 25 was 16%.

But such statistics are rather misleading because they don't tell the whole story. They don't include the millions of youngsters who are not in the labor market because they are continuing with their education or are engaged in training programs. If you take those young people into account, the picture is still grim everywhere, but **the U.S. actually comes off as having a worse youth unemployment problem than Europe**.

The most marginalized group of young people are those who not only don't have a job but are no longer in school, either. In the jargon of economists, these are the so-called **NEET**s, youngsters **N**ot in **E**mployment, **E**ducation or **T**raining.

Their numbers have been rising everywhere, but they are especially prevalent in the U.S. According to the Organization for Economic Co-operation and Development (OECD) in Paris, which has the best data on the subject, 14.8% of young Americans qualified as NEETs in the first quarter of 2011 (the most recent period available), up from 12.1% in the same period in 2007. In the E.U. as a whole, the figure was 13.2%, up from 11.5% in 2007.

Within the European numbers there are big variations. In Germany, Austria and the four Scandinavian countries of Denmark, Sweden, Norway and Finland, the figure is below 10%." *

(*Note that all these countries have socialized healthcare.)

"Spain and Greece have high rates, as would be expected, of 17.6% and 18.2%, respectively, but the worst performer in Europe is actually Italy, with 19.5% of young people out of work and no longer in school or training.

Several factors set apart the countries with a relatively low proportion of NEETs. They all have particularly *extensive* professional training programs for young people. Germany's apprenticeship schemes are the best known; they start early, at age 15 or 16, and mix classroom time with practical experience on the factory floor. The training lasts between one and a half and three years, and by the time they finish, most apprentices move straight into full-time employment. Some of them even end up as CEOs — Hermann Josef Strenger of the chemical giant Bayer, for example.

These nations also have state-funded higher-education systems that are virtually free, and so students have no need to go into debt, unlike in the U.S. And some of the Scandinavian nations, like Denmark, act tough with young people who refuse to participate in training programs — including reducing or cutting their unemployment benefits.

On the other hand, the figures are so high for Greece and Spain in part because, compared with the U.S. and many of their European neighbors, a smaller proportion of young people are actually on the job market — about 30%, compared with 55% in the U.S.

"An unemployment rate of over 50% in Greece and Spain only indicates what is occurring among a relatively small fraction of the total youth population. If the other Greek and Spanish youth were, for example, participating in higher education, there would be less concern about their economic fortunes," says Francis Fong, economist at the Canadian firm TD Economics, in a note that explains the NEET phenomenon. "Focusing solely on the unemployment rate can give an inflated view of the distress among the entire youth population.'

So why are young people in the U.S. so affected by this phenomenon? Jacob Funk Kirkegaard, a research fellow at the Peterson Institute for International Economics, says the NEET numbers probably reflect the depth of the labor-market contraction in the U.S. during the financial crisis, which has actually been worse than in parts of Europe. At the same time, "American youth have fewer education and training opportunities than in Europe — especially following the dramatic cuts to U.S. state and local government education budgets during the crisis."

Akil Holmes wrote the second article recently for polymic. com. It reinforces the need to shift the focus of U.S. education to the practical consideration of securing jobs.

Want to Solve Youth Unemployment? Give Us the Skills to Pay the Bills

"A report released in April of this year by the public policy think tank Demos used 2012 Department of Labor data to analyze the future labor prospects for young Americans. Their analysis discovered that the late 2000s financial crisis exacerbated prior human-capital-development deficiencies, contributed to increased income inequality, and may lead to many long-lasting negative economic and social effects.

High youth unemployment isn't just a problem here in the United States. Youth around the world are unwillingly delaying adulthood because of current global economic conditions. The financial crisis exacerbated the symptoms of unfriendly youth-employment policies practiced by some countries, such as Japan. Job contractions caused educated young adults to increasingly compete for low-paying jobs with more experienced professionals, forcing many to accept positions that do not even require a college degree in order to just make ends meet. **Current youth unemployment and underemployment do not only have short-run negative economic effects, they may affect future income and productivity levels, as young workers do not receive the skills, training, and extra income they would have received if they were put to more efficient use. If policymakers, businesses, and educators do not effectively respond to current youth unemployment by improving skills training and employment opportunities for teenagers and young adults, the country will become more economically and socially divided and continually lose productive capacity.**

The rise of U.S. unemployment in the late 2000s coincided with a seemingly proportional rise in youth unemployment. The rise in

217

overall unemployment suggests a slacker labor market where older, more experienced workers compete with less experienced young adults. Millions of individuals lost their jobs during the last recession and were forced to accept positions that paid drastically less than their previous jobs. It's not surprising that young Americans with college degrees are shut out from having careers until the market improves. If the labor market is bad for college graduates, less educated young adults stand to face an even harder time finding employment. Sustained unemployment has negative effects on a young worker's future earnings and costs society in the form of lost production, higher welfare demand, and higher crime rates.

Skills development has been seen as an important tool for addressing youth employment. With young Americans graduating from college in larger numbers, wages have generally remained low following the end of the early 2000s tech bubble, which suggests wages are being suppressed by an excess of college-educated labor. **The fact that college graduates from different majors have diverging rates of unemployment and that the country faces labor shortages in certain high-paying key industries despite increasing graduation rates suggests inefficient human capital development. Germany is noted as a country that adequately facilitates skill development for its youth, where a long tradition of vocational education and apprenticeships have helped keep youth unemployment down while its European neighbors with no such training structures in place suffer higher rates of youth unemployment.** Management professor at the Wharton School of Business Peter Cappelli also noted that employers also spend less time and money training their workers, which suggests employers favor replacing workers over investing in them.

The youth unemployment problem requires a concerted effort between educators, businesses, and policymakers to correct. **Germany's emphasis on vocational training serves as a good model for the U.S. More young Americans need to be given the opportunity to develop vocational skills before they graduate high school. Employers should increasingly partner with high schools, trade schools, and universities to recruit, train, and hire young adults. There needs to be a better job of pinpointing industries with labor shortages and actively developing the human capital needed to fill these positions. If young adults are more aware of which industries have labor shortages, the number of young Americans graduating from college in over-saturated disciplines might self correct. Policymakers can aid in this process by offering businesses incentives to hire and train young workers through tax breaks and similar programs. The current employment situation for young adults is the natural result of a loose labor market and inefficient human capital development. In order to address to these problems action must now be taken to put young workers to more efficient use, and better prepare future generations for competition in the labor market."**

The last article was written by Denise Deveau for the Canadian Financial Post. **Although it addresses Canadian post-secondary education, it supports my argument that the U.S. educational process must be streamlined and redesigned to create meaningful and long-lasting jobs.**

Canada must streamline education to turn degrees into jobs

"Look at any community college application list, and more

often than not, you'll find a sizable contingent of university graduates. The thought that a university degree is the ticket to instant career success is creating a backlash in Canada. **We have more BAs than the market will bear, a growing shortage of practical skills, and an army of kids burdened with huge debt loads after spending upward of seven years in post-secondary education.**

"We're seeing a lot of university students with generalist degrees going to college to get practical, hands-on, experiential skills," says Donnalee Bell, senior consultant with the Canadian Career Development Foundation in Ottawa. "They have to do that to have better access to jobs."

At the Northern Alberta Institute of Technology (NAIT) in Edmonton, only 20% of students are directly out of high school, reports President and chief executive, Glenn Feltham. Of the remaining 80%, half have prior post-secondary experience.

The overabundance of general degree graduates in Canada has led to dismal underemployment figures, Ms. Bell explains. "What statistics don't tell you is that the system is churning out more BAs than we can possibly absorb. In fact, OECD [Organization for Economic Co-operation and Development] ranks Canada as No. 2 in underemployment of youth. Only Spain is ahead at 50%."

This suggests a large number of Canadian youth are getting jobs for which they are overqualified. "That's not something to be proud of," she says. "We should be asking ourselves, is that really the best we can do in Canada?"

The Scandinavian countries, Germany, Switzerland and Australia have produced much better employment outcomes.

Ironically, these are also regions where the number of students graduating with university degrees is far lower (typically 20% to 30% depending on the country).

The strength of their education systems lies in the fact that the role of employers is infused in the educational process so career pathways are explicitly apparent, she says. To that end, they are very much involved in training and curriculum development. "The focus is on a more direct link to the labor market, so it's not so heavily weighted on the university system.

"We just don't do that here."

Canada needs to start having discussions around career education and what that means in this economic environment, Ms. Bell contends. "We should be helping students connect the pieces to hone their skills and building networks that will parlay them into where to take the next step.

"Universities and colleges need to think about how what they're providing translates into the labor market. And business needs to tell us what skills they need, because we don't know."

Colleges and universities have been making efforts in that direction. In addition to the traditional co-op programs and summer internships, some schools have established articulation agreements or 2+2 programs, which allow students to pursue a hybrid university-college education within a condensed time frame. For example, instead of four years of university and three years of college, they're able to offer students a comparable education with two years of study at each institution, allowing them to enter the workforce sooner and at a lower cost. But

experts say the approach needs to expand further into the system, especially on the university side.

Some are highly creative in their approach. At Memorial University's Faculty of Education, a new initiative called Career Integrated Learning is predicated on the fact that **95% of students going to university don't even know what they want to do,** explains Rob Shea, assistant professor. "That elongates how long they spend in college and university."

The new initiative introduces competencies into course work by refining critical thinking skills through presentations, evaluations, group work and research. The plan is to identify them in every course so graduates in any discipline can better understand and convey those competencies in a job interview.

This cross-pollination of skills can just as easily be applied to the college system, Mr. Shea says. "A student graduating as a mechanic now needs to know technology, bookkeeping, leadership skills, government relationships and communications."

Since 2003, Nova Scotia Community College in Halifax has instituted a portfolio requirement as part of its programs. The artifact portfolio is developed with the help of a faculty member and includes articles, project work, test results, pictures, reflections and other "evidence" of a person's knowledge and competencies for potential employers.

The idea is to take a student's knowledge base and make it real for the workplace, says Laurie Edwards, director of career and counseling services. "When they graduate, they're more 'sellable' to the employer and much more effective in their jobs."

Career planning can be done even sooner to avoid potential over-investment in post secondary education. Janet Uchacz-Hart, executive director for the Saskatoon Industry-Education Council works with school divisions, First Nations communities and industry to give young people exposure to different professions. Through internships, academic placements and conversations with professionals, it provides access to 31 different industries ranging from trades and IT to esthetics and health care.

"When young people find their passion, they're more engaged, motivated and interested in being on time and working in groups," Ms. Uchacz-Hart says. She believes organizations that work with young people are the ones that will survive in the end. "They have a leg up in terms of sustainability, because they understand what youth is all about. It also makes those kids good employees down the road."

While efforts such as these are commendable, they are far from pervasive, says Paul Smith, executive director for the Canadian Association of Career Educators and Employers. **"The roles of colleges and universities in helping students find a way into their first job is not clearly defined."**

The need to find that definition is pressing. Employers, particularly in resource and banking and finance, are having an increasingly difficult time finding the right skill sets, he says. "These are the wealth generators who aren't getting enough of the right people. To them, the notion of hiring and training people up is extremely risky. They want someone who can show up and be billable."

Canadian society needs to change its attitude, Mr. Feltham

says. In reality the dominant pathways to jobs tend to be skills, not university-related credentials. In looking at best practices worldwide, a glaring need identified at NAIT was improving the pathways into and from trades.

Last fall, it introduced a Trades to Degrees program in which a certified skilled trades person can enter the third year of a business degree program. "Industry desperately needs people who can lead others in projects while having a fundamental understanding of how things are produced. It's natural for a trades person to take a business degree because they already have advanced math and business skills," Mr. Feltham says.

The reality, however, is that most leading business schools will accept a person with two years of university-level general arts education into a third-year business program. But a highly skilled trades-person who has spent time in a post-secondary program would have to take a business degree from scratch, which would mean a total of seven years of education.

"Canada needs to build these types of pathways to further education," he says. "The country will be far better off for having these discussions."

In an article written in March 2013 for Borderzine. com, Yurizky Ramos provides the following statistics:

"About 80 percent of students in the United States end up changing their major at least once, according to the National Center for Education Statistics. On average, college students change their major at least three times over the course of their college career."

Question 98: **Do you agree that children should be tested in their early teens to determine their diverse aptitudes and interests and that they should then be streamlined into suitable educational and/or other programs designed for them to succeed?**

Yes___ No___ Undecided___

Question 99: **Do you agree that young people with the requisite interests and skill sets should be placed into apprenticeships and work-study programs that provide "real life" experience and prepare them for long-term suitable jobs and careers?**

Yes___ No___ Undecided

CHAPTER 10
SOME NOT-SO- RANDOM THOUGHTS ON CONTENTIOUS ISSUES

By now, you probably agree that major changes are needed to put an end to political corruption, curb the greed that is rampant within the financial and banking systems, create jobs and introduce a workable healthcare system. I expect that you also support the concept of reducing the disparity between the incomes taken by many business leaders and the salaries and wages paid to employees. No doubt, you can see that a major shift in our nation's educational system is required to assist more young people in becoming productive members of our great society; and many of you are likely in favor of pension and tax reform.

You may not agree with some of my recommendations. If so, let's put some viable alternatives on the table. Arriving at a consensus is the first step in the effecting change.

I believe that there is nothing sacred about the past- certainly when circumstances have rendered the old ways obsolete.

Every nation needs a leader. Perhaps my most radical suggestion is that our President should automatically become the individual who leads the party with the greatest number of seats in the House of Representatives.

Article 2 of The United States Constitution creates the office of the President. *However, the Constitution can be amended.* The original Constitution of the United States was written in 1788. The Bill of Rights included the first 10 amendments and was added to it in 1791. Over the years, there have been 17 additional amendments. The 18th amendment introduced the prohibition of alcohol and the 21st amendment repealed it.

My point is that, so far, the **topics** I have discussed are not likely, in and of themselves, to "push any hot buttons" for the *average American*. Of course, if you are a politician who regularly accepts money from lobbyists, or if you are a hedge fund manager or a CEO of a Fortune 500 company who is paid mega-bucks for moving jobs offshore, you probably aren't going to support many of my recommendations.

However, there are also certain issues that generate strong emotions and our views on these are not necessarily determined by our relative financial standings. More than anything else, these are the issues that divide our country.

Our nation's elected representatives were historically chosen to represent the people *because it was deemed impossible for the people to represent themselves*. **Technology has changed the rules of the game.** In this chapter, I am therefore recommending that these *contentious issues* be put to binding country-wide referendums.

As a nation, we need to address these issues once and for all and we must come to a consensus on each. No matter what, we cannot let ongoing debates tear us apart. In the immortal words of Jesus, repeated by Abraham Lincoln in 1858, **"A house divided against itself cannot stand"**.

What I want to accomplish in this chapter is to simply raise these "hot button" topics. In most cases, I'll present my personal views and my arguments to support these views, but I'm sure there will be many who subscribe to different viewpoints. Nevertheless, one way or another, as difficult as it may be, decisions must be made. In some cases, I believe it will become necessary to get all 50 states to agree to abide by the will of the majority in order to set *a uniform policy across the country.*

At the end of this chapter, I will pose questions on which I ask you to cast your vote. Remember, you will remain anonymous. I look forward to seeing the results and I hope you do too.

There have been many polls on some of these issues, but I fear that, in some cases, the people who were asked to respond were selected from a population base that may have been biased. I'd like to believe that I am reaching a broad cross-section of our society, representing different values and beliefs.

The topics I have selected for "discussion" are:

1. Environmental issues

2. The role of the U.S. Military in our society

3. Gun control

4. Separation of Church and State - Can we end our religious differences?

5. Pro Choice vs. Pro Life – the abortion controversy

6. Gay rights

7. The death penalty

Environmental issues

Anyone living in this country who hasn't been asleep for the past 25 years or so understands the need for recycling. Our government has created agencies like the Environmental Protection Agency (EPA) to regulate pollution issues and to balance business objectives with the concerns of environmentalists. Logging, mining and oil & gas are good examples of industries that are overseen by these agencies.

In January 2012, Yale and Columbia Universities issued a study called "The Environmental Performance Index" that ranked 132 countries. The United States came in 49th, while China ranked 116th and India 125th. While the U.S. didn't quite finish in the top one-third, I believe it is noteworthy that many of the leading countries have much smaller populations and are far less industrialized.

Examples include Costa Rica, Iceland Luxembourg and New Zealand.

All in all, I have no major suggestions to make with respect to improving our nation's efforts at becoming more environmentally friendly. I'd like to see less packaging for most goods but I also understand the necessity for advertising and (sadly) the need to "bulk up" products on retailers' shelves to prevent theft.

I stressed early on that I believe we need to clean up (pun intended) our own house before we turn our attention to the world at large. However, there is one question I'd like to pose:

Do you believe that the United States should impose trading sanctions on countries that refuse to make a concerted effort to become more environmentally friendly?

This is not an easy question to answer. I came across an interesting article recently entitled "Why the iPad has to be Made in China" on ifixit.org. I've reproduced excerpts from it below.

"The iPad's light, sleek, simple construction belies its complex origins. There's a lot of stuff in the iPad: aluminum and glass, of course, but also other heavy metals and toxic chemicals. **And manufacturing each 1.44-pound iPad results in over 285 times its own weight in greenhouse gas emissions**. The manufacturing of and material used in the iPad are two reasons why the iPad must be made in China—and not just in the ways you'd expect.

Yes, labor is dirt cheap in China. Minimum wage was just $138/month at Hongkai Electronics in October 2010, compared to $1160/month in the US (based on a $7.25/hour federal minimum wage and a 40-hour work week).

But there's another important reason why Apple and other manufacturers have their heels stuck in Chinese mud. iPad manufacturing, like the manufacturing of other electronics, requires a significant amount of rare earth elements, the 17 difficult-to-mine elements used in all kinds of technology. It's hard to say exactly what rare earths are in an iPad, since Apple is really tight-lipped about their materials—no one can even get them to confirm what manufacturer makes their impact-resistant glass.

Why is all this rare earth consumption a problem? China currently controls 95-97% of the world's supply of rare earths and has repeatedly cut export quotas, sending already-high prices skyrocketing. Fearing dependence on China for rare earths, two companies—Molycorp in California and Lynas Corp in Australia—plan to begin mining rare earths this year. As green industry continues to grow, however, it's unclear if current mining operations will be able to keep up with increasing demand.

Facing growing concern about the possibility of a rare earth shortage, President Obama recently lodged a complaint with the World Trade Organization against China about their rare earth policy. Some specialists think the complaint may be too little too late—by the time China changes its policy, more manufacturers will have moved plants to China.

Today, an American electronics company can only be exempt from China's rare earth export quotas by manufacturing within China. So that's what most companies, including Apple,

are doing. **The only other solution is for us to stop consuming so much—an option that people rarely find appealing. Not as appealing as a retina display, at least."**

I love my iPad more than you can imagine. It has saved me countless research hours and I use it constantly for banking, monitoring my credit cards, reading books and playing Sudoku and Hearts. (Yes, I do have a life away from my iPad too!)

Would I pay double for it if it were manufactured here? I refuse to answer...

The role of the U.S. Military in our society

When I was 12, my family moved from New York City to Montreal, Canada. When I reached the age of 18, I registered for the U.S. draft. Since I was a legitimate resident of a foreign country, my registration was processed through a special draft board in Washington D.C. That board had a zero quota, so I was never called up; I didn't even have to apply for a student deferment while in university.

Would I have gone had they called my number? I don't know. I'm pretty sure I would have been classified as unfit due to extremely poor vision and/or hearing problems. Loud music or noises can make my ears ring for days. I have never shot a starter's pistol, let alone a real firearm.

Anyway, I have no military experience whatsoever, but I still think I can provide some valid and objective comments based on what I've seen, heard and read over many years.

I believe that the last time the United States actually won a war was in 1945. How did we win? We released the atom bomb on Hiroshima and Nagasaki and the Japanese capitulated. We also bombed Dresden and Cologne to the ground and Germany surrendered. If you get a chance, take a look on the Internet at pictures of the damages sustained by these last two cities. The allies bombed Cologne on 262 separate occasions. There was no need to resort to atomic warfare.

By using aerial attacks, we were able to finally put an end to the war in the European Theater and save thousands of U.S. lives in the process. No one worried too much about "**collateral damage**" back then. According to Wikipedia, that term only started being used in 1961.

The Korean War, which began in 1950, has technically never ended. A cease-fire in 1953 tacitly terminated overt hostilities. The war in Vietnam that started about 10 years later was the first one brought into our homes on T.V. in living color. It finally ended as a result of negotiations-nobody surrendered. Over 58,000 young lives were terminated prematurely as a result of the U.S. policy to continue to deploy ground troops and to structure bombing missions designed to avoid civilian targets. Many of our surviving troops were traumatized for life and large numbers were abandoned by society. Many are homeless and traumatized to this very day.

In my opinion, ground warfare is obsolete. You

cannot send troops into areas where many inhabitants are hostile, and where you can't tell the "good guys" from the "bad guys", without incurring substantial losses.

In years gone by, the rationale for American military policy was to keep the world safe from Communism. Well, that era is over. Ironically, the last survivor of the Cold War Era is Fidel Castro, the leader of a backward and impoverished country. Capitalism is gradually being adopted by the Eastern European Bloc countries and in China. Unfortunately, the model seems to be even more pronounced Unbridled Capitalism than we are experiencing in America. If anything, any movement in the United States towards Enlightened Capitalism should serve as a role model for other countries to emulate.

Now we face another enemy- Militant Islam and its terrorist groups. **Can we really expect to stamp out terrorism with ground troops? I don't believe we can. Are there other ways? Maybe.**

Why do many devout Moslems hate us? The first Gulf War began in 1990 after Iraq invaded Kuwait. The U.S. quickly stepped in and invaded Iraq. Was the reason based on altruistic motives-to act as a peacemaker and help the downtrodden? Or was the primary motive to protect U.S oil interests in the Middle East? The answer actually doesn't matter any more. The U.S. forced Sadaam Hussein to back down fairly quickly. Contrary to his commanding general's advice, former President George H.W. Bush refused to advance to and occupy Baghdad. The President must have felt that he had accomplished his objective to restore peace and stability to the area and that it was better to walk away.

However, the by-product of our entry into the Middle East was to foster a marked escalation of hatred against the United States, which had been fomenting since 1948 when the U.S. supported the formation of the State of Israel. (I'm not suggesting that the U.S. shouldn't support Israel. Live and let live.)

This militant Islamic hatred boiled over in September 2001. After the initial shock, former President George W. Bush felt that he needed to retaliate. He chose Iraq and Sadaam Hussein as his target. Why? Well, we were told Sadaam had weapons of mass destruction. Did he? No. Was Mr. Bush's information *that seriously flawed*? The CIA didn't even attempt to plant weapons of mass destruction to justify American actions!

Personally, I think Mr. Bush had two underlying reasons to target Iraq. The first was that he succumbed to the prodding of U.S. oil interests, spearheaded by his VP Dick Cheney. The second was a personal desire to rectify the "mistake" his father had made ten years earlier by stopping short of invading Baghdad. In my opinion, he simply wanted to get out from under his father's shadow and prove his own self-worth.

In the final analysis, we learned that it was Saudi Nationals –our so-called allies- who perpetrated the 9/11 attacks. Maybe Sadaam was a "bad guy", but was it really our business to take him down?

I recently read that the costs of the Second Iraq war amounted to about $1 Trillion. 4,487 soldiers were killed and 32,223 were seriously wounded. In the aftermath, about 30% of our veterans developed serious mental health problems. The current unemployment percentage of Gulf War veterans is estimated at 9.9%

Yes, Sadaam Hussein is dead and so is Osama Bin Laden. But will there be a lasting peace in Iraq? Bombings and violent acts continue to be almost an every-day occurrence and the Sunnis and Shiites continue to murder each other.

Let's just assume for the moment that the second Gulf war was justified and let me ask a couple of rhetorical questions. (No need to vote!)

What would have happened if George W. Bush had told Sadaam from the get go that he had 48 hours to surrender himself and his Republican Guard, or the U.S. would level Baghdad to the ground? What if Mr. Bush would have followed through on his threat and had refused to consider "collateral damage" (assuming Sadaam either refused to surrender and/or failed to evacuate all civilians in time)?

I'm **not** suggesting that this is what Mr. Bush should have done. *All I'm trying to do is to emphasize my personal belief that ground warfare is virtually obsolete.* Yes, we need a national guard to protect us if we are ever attacked on our own soil. But do we need to train ground troops to the same extent as we did many years ago? When these people leave the military, are most of them well suited for civilian jobs?

I suggested in Chapter 3 that a peacetime draft should be instituted to take in young unemployed or underemployed Americans and use them to repair and build infrastructure construction projects, such as roads and bridges, while also training them for a variety of post-draft jobs and careers.

This whole issue is not an easy one to resolve. The United States is operating with a huge accumulated deficit, a large chunk of which can be attributed to military spending. With this in mind, I raise one further question on this issue for you to consider:

Do you believe military spending budgets should be cut where reasonably possible, with a major portion of the savings allocated to fund both the civilian training of young people as well as a workable healthcare system?

Gun control

"A well regulated militia being necessary to the security of a free State, the right of the People to keep and bear arms shall not be infringed."

Second Amendment to the Unites States
Constitution

It amazes me that the meaning of two lines, both containing relatively simple everyday words, should elicit a controversy that has spanned several centuries. There are two common interpretations.

The interpretation that is most widely accepted is that our Founding Fathers simply bestowed a legacy upon the American people giving them the right to keep and bear arms.

Another interpretation hinges upon the fact that, in the early years of our country, individuals were generally expected to supply their own weapons if and when called upon to protect our nation's security. This interpretation emphasizes the first thirteen words of the amendment that prefaces the entire statement with reference to "a well regulated militia."

Whatever the intention might have been, it is obvious to me that our Founding Fathers couldn't possibly conceive of the concept that a simple musket would evolve one day into a weapon that could fire up to 60 rounds per minute.

Times change and I believe we must have the willingness to adapt with the times. The Old Testament forbade the consumption of pork products and shellfish. Yet today, Christians and most Jews ignore this prohibition. This restriction was introduced at a time long before the invention of refrigeration and modern day sanitation and is no longer relevant.

The Catholic Church astounded many of its adherents in the 1960s when the centuries-old prohibition against eating meat on Fridays was revoked. It was viewed as being no longer necessary for the Church to protect the livelihood of fishermen.

The issue of prohibition sets a precedent for repealing an amendment and the existence of amendments themselves proves that the actual Constitution itself can be amended.

Be that as it may, **there is a very large percentage of Americans who believe no one has any right to take their firearms away.**

Therefore, only three alternatives exist.

1. Keep the status-quo
2. Revoke the right of persons who are not in law enforcement to bear arms other than those suitable for hunting
3. Some sort of compromise.

Many Americans are aware that Canada has gun control laws. If you have ever traveled to Canada or planned a trip, you know that it is illegal to bring firearms into the country. However, what you might not know is that gun *control* is not the same as the confiscation of all firearms.

Below is an excerpt from the Royal Canadian Mounted Police (RCMP) publication that explains Canada's gun control policies.

"There are three classes of firearms: non-restricted, restricted and prohibited.

Non-restricted firearms are ordinary rifles and shotguns, other than those referred to below.

Restricted firearms include:

- handguns that are not prohibited;

- semi-automatic, center-fire rifles and shotguns with a barrel shorter than 470 mm;

- rifles and shotguns that can be fired when their overall length has been reduced by folding, telescoping or other means to less than 660 mm; and

- firearms restricted by *Criminal Code Regulations.*

Prohibited firearms include:

- handguns with a barrel length of 105 mm or less and handguns that discharge .25 or .32 caliber ammunition, except for a few specific ones used in International Shooting Union competitions;

- rifles and shotguns that have been **altered** by sawing or other means so that their barrel length is less than 457 mm or their overall length is less than 660 mm;

- full automatics;

- converted automatics, namely full automatics that have been altered so that they fire only one projectile when the trigger is squeezed; and

- firearms prohibited by *Criminal Code Regulations.*"

The Canada Firearms Act provides a legal framework whereby an individual may acquire, possess and carry a restricted or (a specific class of) prohibited firearm for protection from other individuals *when police protection is deemed insufficient.* This situation is extremely rare. The allowance refers only to protection of life during employment that involves handling of valuable goods or dangerous wildlife.

There are also rules in Canada requiring attendance at a training program in order to obtain any firearms whatsoever as well as registration of all firearms even if not restricted.

I know that there have been studies in many countries dealing with relative crime rates before and after gun control legislation was passed. There are also studies comparing violent crime rates in countries where there is gun control and where there isn't. I'm not sure they are either conclusive or, for that matter, relevant.

There are many people in Canada who are unhappy with the concept of gun control and I'd bet that there are still many illegal and non-registered weapons in circulation.

In any event, I believe my personal feeling about this issue is irrelevant but also, so is the opinion of any of our elected representatives.

I recommend that this issue be resolved by way of a binding nation-wide referendum, coinciding with an upcoming Presidential election to ensure the greatest voter turnout. I also recommend that the issues be summarized clearly in a two or three page document written in language we can all understand.

I am adding two questions on this topic to my poll;

1. Do you believe that the United States government should establish a general class of prohibited weapons that includes full automatics and other firearms more likely than not to be used primarily to assist in committing crimes?

2. Do you believe that a binding nation-wide referendum should be held on the issue of gun control?

Separation of Church and State - Can we end our religious differences?

"Congress shall make no law respecting an establishment of religion, or prohibiting the free exercise thereof:"

The first clause in the First Amendment to the United States Constitution

"So anybody here today who has not accepted Jesus Christ as their savior, I'm telling you, you're not my brother and you're not my sister, and I want to be your brother."

Robert Bentley, Alabama Governor –Elect,
January 17, 2011

Although Mr. Bentley quickly apologized for his remarks, statements like his scare the **hell** out of me. (Perhaps that is what he intended.)

In 1802, Thomas Jefferson made it clear in a letter to the Danbury Baptist Association that the First Amendment was designed in part to **separate church and state**. (The First Amendment also guarantees the rights of free speech, freedom of the press and peaceable assembly.)

We are a very diverse country with many different viewpoints on the existence of God, evolution vs. creationism and organized religion. There is no point for me to make any attempt to provide percentages. What little research I was able to track down shows me that the numbers vary dramatically, depending on how the poll parameters were selected.

There are people who follow an established religion, people who believe in God but do not adhere to the practices of any religion and do not attend services or pray, and there are atheists and agnostics. In my opinion, the only "law" that applies to all of us is "**Do unto others as you would have then do unto you.**"

Over the ages, most wars were started for either economic reasons (such as to claim territory) or for religious reasons, or both. History chronicles Crusades, Inquisitions and Pogroms. In more recent times, we witnessed Hitler's obsession with wiping out the Jews and genocide in several African countries.

Today, there are Moslem sects who fight each other in Iraq and Orthodox Jews who throw stones at Secular Jews who drive their cars in Jerusalem on the Sabbath. **Many, many wars were based on the premise that "My God is better than yours, and, if you don't believe me, I'll kill you!"**

It may surprise you, but the only other *species* in the world that goes to war besides man is colonies of **ants**. Red ants hate black ants and vice versa. It is true that there are fights to the death among many kinds of creatures. Two male lions may fight over a female or there may be an isolated dispute over territory or prey, but you'll never see an out-and-out war.

All I can hope for is religious tolerance. **In my opinion, tolerance is a Cardinal Rule of Enlightenment. In the eyes of the law, we are all created equal.**

I'll pose another question in my poll:

Do you believe that we must practice religious tolerance in the United States and refrain from making any unwelcome attempts to coerce others to follow specific religious beliefs?

I do have one additional related item on my wish list. **I would like to see a non-aggression accord between the United States and all of the Islamic countries, whereby the U.S. agrees not to intervene in their domestic issues unless we are invited to do so in the role of peacemakers by the presiding government of a particular country. In exchange, I would require that the Islamic countries fully support our efforts to wipe out global terrorism. This accord would grant all legitimate Muslim residents and citizens of the United States freedom from discrimination.**

World Peace. In Shakespeare's words (although in a different context): "t'is a consummation devoutly to be wished."

Gay Rights

Below is a summary of a 2011 study authored by Dr. Gary J. Gates of The Williams Institute- the University Of California School Of Law:

"Drawing on information from four recent national and two state-level population-based surveys, the analyses suggest that there are more than 8 million adults in the US who are lesbian, gay, or bisexual, comprising 3.5% of the adult population. In total, the study suggests that approximately 9 million Americans – roughly the population of New Jersey – identify as LGBT.

Among adults who identify as lesbian, gay, or bisexual, bisexuals comprise a slight majority (1.8% compared to 1.7% who identify as lesbian or gay); women are substantially more likely than men to identify as bisexual; estimates of those who report any lifetime same-sex sexual behavior and any same-sex sexual attraction are substantially higher than estimates of those who identify as lesbian, gay, or bisexual. There are also nearly 700,000 transgender individuals in the US. An estimated 19 million Americans (8.2%) report that they have engaged in same-sex sexual behavior and nearly 25.6 million Americans (11%) acknowledge at least some same-sex sexual attraction."

I believe that any debate on the numbers or percentages is counter-productive. *The point is that the numbers are significant.* Personally, I believe in equal rights for lesbians, gays, bisexuals and transgendered people. I think any attempt to "change" them is ludicrous. I believe they should have the same right to marry as heterosexuals and that they should not be discriminated against in any way.

For those who quote the Bible as the source of their condemnation of homosexuality, I ask that they refrain from eating pork products and shellfish; that they should practice animal sacrifices and avoid all garments that are made from mixed fibers. Clearly there are many laws in the Old Testament that appear ridiculous to us in the 21st Century. Hatred and/or disdain for homosexuality is probably tops on **my** list.

But, yet again, my views don't matter. We cannot let this issue hold us back.

I recommend a nation-wide binding referendum on the issue of gay marriage and on the right of gays and lesbians to raise children.

Pro Choice vs. Pro Life – the Abortion Controversy

Of all the issues I raise in this chapter, I believe this one is the most difficult to resolve. There is no doubt that taking a life is generally unacceptable. Obviously, if one is fighting a war, the choice is often to kill or be killed. Only 18 States and the District of Columbia have abolished the death penalty, which I will discuss next. Most of them are therefore still open to discussion whether or not there should be a policy of "an eye for an eye". But, obviously an unborn is not a criminal whose acts *might* support legalized execution.

At some point a child becomes a human life. Whether it is at the time of conception, after a certain number of weeks or months of gestation, or at the time of birth is open for discussion. Most religious groups are very opposed to abortion. They favor the alternative of adoption,

Standing on the other side of the "scale" are those who believe that every woman is entitled to decide whether or not she wishes to bear a child. There are some who would support a woman's right to an abortion only if her life might be compromised or if medical testing of the fetus reveals mental or physical deformities.

Personally, I don't believe that anyone has the right to force a woman to bear a child against her wishes. But, again, I believe this issue should be dealt with by way of a nation-wide referendum. The questions I will pose in my poll are:

1. Are you totally against legalizing abortions under any circumstances?

2. Would you support legalized abortion if the prospective mother's life or long-term health were at risk?

3. Would you support legalized abortion if medical testing reveals mental or physical deformities in the unborn child?

4. Do you believe that every woman is entitled to decide whether or not she   wishes to bear a child?

The Death Penalty

There is likely nothing I can tell you about the pros and cons of the death penalty that you don't already know.

My poll questions that I believe should ultimately be considered by way of referendum are:

1. Should the death penalty be abolished completely?

2. Should the death penalty apply as a possible sentence when someone is convicted of murdering a police officer or public official?

3. Should the death penalty apply as a possible sentence when someone is convicted of mass murder?

4. If the death penalty is accepted by referendum, should the sentence be carried out within 24 months?

In conclusion, I would like to reiterate the reasons why I selected the "hot button" topics that I covered in this chapter. I believe most of them are easily capable of polarizing our country. **I would not like to see a framework whereby any American votes for a particular person or party** *solely based on that person's or party's views on one or more of these topics.* **That is why I heartily recommend that they be handled by referendum.**

Question100: **Do you believe that the United States government should impose trading sanctions on countries that refuse to make a concerted effort to become more environmentally friendly?**

Yes___ No___ Undecided___

Question 101: **Do you agree that ground warfare is largely obsolete?**

Yes___ No___ Undecided___

Question 102: **Do you agree that military spending budgets should be cut where reasonably possible, with a major portion of the savings allocated to fund both the civilian training of young people as well as implementing a workable healthcare system?**

Yes___ No___ Undecided___

Question 103: **Do you agree that the United States government should establish a general class of prohibited weapons that includes full automatics and other firearms more likely than not to be used primarily to assist in committing crimes?**

Yes____ No____ Undecided____

Question 104: **Do you believe that a binding nation-wide referendum should be held on the issue of gun control?**

Yes____ No____ Undecided____

Question 105: **Do you agree that we must practice religious tolerance in the United States and refrain from making any unwelcome attempts to coerce others to follow specific religious beliefs?**

Yes____ No____ Undecided____

Question 106: **Do you agree that there should be a nation-wide binding referendum on the issue of gay marriage and on the right of gays and lesbians to raise children?**

Yes____ No____ Undecided____

Question 107:   **Are you totally against legalizing abortions under any circumstances?**

Yes___ No___ Undecided___

Question 108: **Would you support legalized abortion if the prospective mother's life or long-term health were at risk?**

Yes___ No___ Undecided___

Question 109: **Would you support legalized abortion if medical testing reveals mental or physical deformities in the unborn child?**

Yes___ No___ Undecided___

Question 110: **Do you believe that every woman is entitled to decide whether or not she wishes to bear a child?**

Yes___ No___ Undecided___

Question 111: **Should the death penalty be completely abolished?**

Yes___ No___ Undecided___

Question 112: **Should the death penalty apply as a possible sentence when someone is convicted of murdering a police officer or public official?**

Yes___ No___ Undecided___

Question 113: **Should the death penalty apply as a possible sentence when someone is convicted of mass murder?**

Yes___ No___ Undecided___

Question 114: **If the death penalty is accepted by referendum, should the sentence be carried out within 24 months?**

Yes___ No___ Undecided___

CHAPTER 11
FINANCIAL EDUCATION AND IMPLEMENTATION- THE KEYS TO YOUR SECURITY

Introduction

The title of this chapter speaks for itself. Social responsibility embraces the concept that we all must all look after ourselves as best we can, so as not to become burdens on our fellow citizens. We must do our best to earn our own livings, stay healthy and be respectful of our environment.

Social responsibility also requires at least some degree of financial awareness. What I am going to do in this last chapter is to explain what every single American should have learned and should be learning in high school. Initially, I will examine the **budgeting process**, where there is little involved other than basic arithmetic.

What then follows is an analysis of what **inflation** means *and what it doesn't mean*. In this chapter, I intend to explode the prevailing myths about inflation and show you that its so-called importance has been greatly overrated by both government and the media.

Then I'll turn to the subject of setting **financial goals**. In the days before the Internet, this was a somewhat difficult issue to deal with-especially for those who have an aversion towards mathematical formulas. Now it's really easy. If you want to know how much money you need to set aside each month to accumulate a targeted amount at the end, you need only pose the question on your favorite search engine and you will be directed to several websites where you can plug in your numbers and see the results.

Finally, we'll move on to **the implementation of a plan,** which involves selecting an advisor. I'll share a few tips that I believe will help.

I hope by now it is obvious to you that most Americans will find the goal of attaining financial security much more easily accomplished if many of the recommendations in this book are adopted.

Budgeting your personal expenses

Generally, you will find this process easiest if you make your calculations on a monthly basis and multiply the total by 12 at the end *if you want a total for the year*. Certain costs are incurred less frequently than monthly, such as property taxes that are often paid in two installments. Just take the total of the two amounts and divide by 12 to get a monthly budget figure.

The reason I suggest monthly figures is because most of us earn our incomes in a way that we can best compare *monthly* inflows and outflows.

My first concrete recommendation is that **you**

should open a separate bank account and make deposits out of each paycheck for major expenses that are not incurred evenly throughout the year. When the time comes to pay them, you can then simply draw the money from this special account.

You should be able to put all your numbers together from your **bank, credit card and debit card statements**.

Here is a **sample budget** that covers almost all circumstances:

Housing

Rent/Mortgage payments   _____

Mortgage principal *   _____

Mortgage interest   _____

Property taxes   _____

Heating   _____

Electricity   _____

Insurance   _____

Maintenance and improvements   _____

Furnishings and appliances   _____

Telephone   _____

Water   _____

TV Cable   _____

Internet   _____

                                                    $_____

Food

At home   _____

Away   _____

                                                    $_____

Transportation

Public transportation   _____

Automobile

Car payments/rentals   _____

Gasoline and oil   _____

Insurance   _____

License   _____

Repairs and maintenance   _____

Tires   _____

                                                    $_____

Clothing

Purchases   _____

Laundry and cleaning   _____

$_____

Recreation, reading and education

Travel and vacations   _____

Club memberships and dues   _____

Miscellaneous   _____

Babysitting/daycare costs   _____

Education costs/tuition fees, room and board etc.

_____

Books and magazines for personal use   _____

Video rentals and other   _____

$_____

Tobacco and alcohol

Tobacco products **   _____

Alcohol   _____

$_____

Health and personal care

Medical and dental insurance premium   _____

Medical/dental services not covered by insurance

_____

Grooming   _____

$ _____

Other

Credit card interest***   _____

Gifts to friends and family

_____

Insurance premiums

Life insurance   _____

Disability insurance   _____

Expenses of pet ownership   _____

Other costs: _____(specify)   _____

$ _____

Total personal expenditures $ _____

===========

*Note that mortgage *principal* payments increase the equity you have in your home.

**If you are a smoker, I strongly recommend that you stop and use the savings to pay down your credit card debt and then your mortgage.

*** Credit card interest can destroy your financial plan. Instead of building *your* net worth, you are increasing the net worth of your bank.

In Chapter 6, I stressed the need for Americans to pay off their home mortgages quickly, even if this means foregoing some tax advantages. I compared the outlays required to pay off a thirty-year mortgage over only fifteen years and showed you the potential interest saving. **Remember, even if you are in a 30% tax bracket, home mortgage interest still costs *you* seventy cents on the dollar!**

Because this is such an important component of building financial security, I am repeating the example here:

The next table calculates the difference between fifteen year financing and thirty year financing of $100,000 at a 5% mortgage rate. If your outstanding mortgage is for $213,000, just multiply the relevant numbers by 2.13.

	30 year mortgage 100,000	15 year mortgage 100,000	Difference
Interest Rate	5%	5%	
Monthly payment	$536.82	$790.79	$253.97
Total Payments	$193,256	$142,342	$50,914
Total Interest	$93,256	$42,342	$50,914

For an extra $250 a month for every $100,000 of financing, you can pay for your home fifteen years earlier, enhance your financial security, and save almost $51,000. For a while, the extra $250 may mean going out for dinner less lavishly or frequently, bringing your lunch to work, having an after-work drink at home instead of at a bar, or choosing a less expensive car to drive. If many of my recommendations are accepted, you are likely to see increases in your disposable income that you can choose earmark towards building more equity in your home.

So, to recap:

1. If you smoke, STOP! You are just burning your money, ruining your health and putting others at risk.

2. Pay off your credit card debt as quickly as you can.

3. Try to amortize your home mortgage over fifteen years even if it means buying a less expensive home.

The inflation myths

Before we examine the concept of inflation, we must first look at the Consumer Price Index. Here is how Wikipedia defines it.

"The **consumer price index (CPI)** measures changes in the price level of a market basket of consumer goods and services purchased by households. The CPI in the United States is defined by the Bureau of Labor Statistics as "a measure of the average change over time in the prices paid by urban consumers for a market basket of consumer goods and services.""

The CPI is a statistical estimate constructed using the prices of a sample of representative items whose prices are collected periodically. Sub-indexes and sub-sub-indexes are computed for different categories and sub-categories of goods and services, being combined to produce the overall index with *weights reflecting their shares in the total of the consumer expenditures covered by the index.* The annual percentage change in a CPI is used as a measure of inflation."

Please note the important concept of **weighting**. Families clearly spend more on some components than on others. Here is the **approximate** average overall breakdown:

Category	Percentage
Housing	**36%**
Food	**17%**
Transportation	**17%**
Clothing	**7%**
Recreation, reading and education	**8%**
Tobacco and alcohol	**5%**
Health and personal care	**10%**
	100%

The first inflation myth is that the published rate of inflation means that all costs are going up (or down) by the same percentage. Let's suppose the government raises taxes by 10% on tobacco and alcohol. That would cause a 10% x 5%= one-half of 1% change in the overall index for that particular month. When the published monthly increase in the CPI is around 1% in total, an increase just from raising taxes on tobacco and alcohol could become statistically important. It may have caused (as in my example) half of the total change. **Clearly, a single change in a component of the index does not mean that all the components are changing equally.**

Another example of the potential significant impact of a change in only one component of the CPI is the price of gasoline at the pump or heating oil that fluctuates on a seasonal basis. Changes in a single component will affect the calculation of the whole index, but they certainly don't mean that everything is changing.

The second and probably most misleading myth is that inflation affects us all equally. If no one in your family smokes or drinks, are you personally affected by changes in the price of tobacco or alcohol? If you live in a large city, walk or bicycle to work and don't own a car, do gasoline prices matter to you?

Every one of us is affected to a greater or lesser extent by inflation, ***depending on our own personal circumstances.*** **Published statistical numbers are sometimes meaningless.** Take the employment statistics as another example. If you have a great job, or own a profitable business, you might still be concerned about unemployment statistics since you care about your fellow citizens, *but they really don't affect you personally.*

Proper financial planning involves calculating your own personal exposure to inflationary forces and taking whatever steps you can to reduce this exposure.

Here is the best example I can give you to show that cost of living numbers are personal and averages here are meaningless. Assume you and your next-door neighbor live in virtually identical homes. You are good friends. One day, you ring your neighbor's doorbell and say, "Congratulate me. I just made my last mortgage payment. I can now save $750 a month."

Your neighbor responds," That's great, but I've got some news too. We just bought a new house and we're going to be moving. Funny, my monthly mortgage payment will be going **UP** by $750 a month."

So, you can see how one family's cost of living can drop while another family's cost of living can increase by the same amount on literally the same day.

The next myth, often perpetrated by government, is that whenever inflation rises rapidly, the blame should be placed on employees and their unions because of unreasonable wage demands.

It is true that overall wage increases will have an impact on increasing inflation. However, *most inflation is caused by government*. The largest single factor that

affects the cost of living index is interest rates, *and it is our government that dictates what the prevailing rate will be.*

Let's assume the prevailing interest rate on home mortgages is 7%. The government then decides to stimulate the economy by lowering this rate to 4%. People all over the country hurry to refinance their homes. Their costs of living drop. (They buy new cars to celebrate.)

On the other hand, what if the government raises interest rates? People who are now required to refinance their homes will find that their living costs are on the rise. They hold back from buying cars or expensive electronics because they cannot afford to do so.

In recent years, in order to kick-start the economy after the 2008 collapse of home prices precipitated a nation-wide banking crisis, the government responded by lowering interest rates to levels I had never seen before in over fifty years. **As a result, the reported inflation numbers have been very low for the last few years.**

As a by-product of this move to save the economy from further decline, many people, who would have been content to earn reasonable rates of interest without having to take significant risks, have been forced into the stock market and its derivatives, such as Exchange Traded Funds.

At the time I am writing this, the U.S. government is threatening to take steps to gradually increase interest rates. However, I have serious doubts about whether they can follow through without collapsing the stock market and greatly reducing the demand for housing and consumer goods.

The next major myth is that inflation is always bad. I would like to postulate that **modest inflation is synonymous with growth.** If everyone believes that costs will rise, they will usually make discretionary expenditures sooner rather than later. This behavior acts as an overall stimulus for the economy. If consumers are buying, manufacturers increase production and hire more people. Deflation has the reverse effect.

The last myth is that we are all exposed to inflation to the same extent throughout our lives from adulthood on.

Take another look at the components of my sample budget. By the time you retire:

1. Your home must be paid for in full and must be in good repair.
2. You must own one or two fully-paid vehicles that you are prepared to keep, if necessary, for the following 15 years.
3. You must try to rid yourself of dependent children or (at least) no longer be paying for their education!

If you do all this, it becomes obvious that your housing and transportation costs will be quite manageable. If you have no dependent children, your food and clothing costs will be a great deal lower than they were previously. In fact, your own clothing costs will probably decline to the extent you no longer require attire suitable for business or work.

If you are a heavy smoker and/or drinker, you

probably won't live all that long and you can afford to have fewer savings. (Many truths are told in jest, as the saying goes.)

The only major variable is recreation. If you are well off, you may choose to travel extensively and/or own a second residence. At the other extreme, you may be forced to stay close to home. Many people downsize their homes to pocket some extra money and/or move to certain retirement areas where the cost of living is reasonably low.

I used to lecture extensively in Canada on financial planning. I held the designation of Certified Financial Planner (CFP). Unfortunately, I had to surrender my CFP when I retired, because the rules of the CFP organization restrict the use of the letters to active practitioners only.

Over the years, I became very unpopular because I told people to pay off their homes. By so doing, I was keeping them away from the clutches of "planners" who made their livings selling mutual funds and other investments. I have no regrets. I still stand behind my advice.

Paying off a home is not glamorous, but I believe you will sleep better at night compared to your friends who are active speculators in the stock market.

The bottom line is that, with proper planning, you can significantly reduce your exposure to rising costs, as you grow older.

Setting financial goals

At the beginning of this chapter, I said that once you have mastered the "fine art" of budgeting (it's really simple once you make up your mind to deal with it) and once you understand the basics of how to control your living costs, I would discuss the topic of setting specific long-term financial goals.

I lied!!!!

In my opinion it is impossible to set r*ealistic* long-term financial goals. Here's why. When, at the age of 20, I entered a program to become a professional accountant, I was required to take a course in mathematics of finance. Once I mastered the material, I made a calculation of how much I would have to save each month for the next 45 years to accumulate $100,000 by age 65.

For someone earning $2,000 a year, $100,000 was a fortune. Established Chartered Accountants were earning about $10,000 a year in Canada at that time. I never dreamed that, by the time I was 35, I'd be earning over $100,000 in a single year.

What does all this mean? Well, one cannot really set any long-term goals, except to pay off one's home, *because the passage of time plays havoc with one's plans.*

There is the futuristic story about a young man who develops a fatal disease at a relatively young age. He is fairly well off and he decides to have his body frozen until medical science can find a way to cure him. He puts his money into a trust administered by a reputable management firm.

Many years later, he is defrosted and awakens to the news that he can now be cured. He asks the person who had thawed him out how much money he was now worth. He was told that his trust amounted to just over $10 Million. "Wow, I'm rich!" he exclaimed. "Well, not really," was the reply, "But you can afford to buy me a cup of coffee, if you'd like."

So, if you can't set goals, what can you do?

The answer comes from understanding the following relationships:

Inflation, Interest rates, Investment yields and Income all tend to move in the same direction at the same time.

I call these the "Four I's". High *I*nterest rates result in high *I*nflation (a more expensive cost of living). If the cost of living goes up, workers demand higher *I*ncomes. Also, when inflation is rising, people buy in order to avoid the next price increase. Businesses make more profits and owners' *I*nvestment yields increase. My example may be a bit simplistic, but I trust you get the picture.

Your financial goal should simply be to set aside a fixed percentage of your income from year-to-year. Initially, that saving should be used to pay down your

mortgage. If there is anything left over, the money should be used fund your childrens' education and maintain an Individual Retirement Account (IRA).

Once your home is paid, it is likely you will be able to put a greater percentage of your income away each year. The percentage will change again once your children are self-supporting and leave the nest.

The initial percentage that I recommend depends in part on your age. Generally, if you are in your early thirties, 10% is a good starting point. *However, the older you are when you start, the greater the required percentage.*

A good analogy will take you back to your student years. Remember the time you had, say, 20 days to prepare for a history final. Your textbook contained 400 pages, so you decided to review 20 pages a day. The first day, something came up, and you told yourself that you could easily start the following day and review 21 pages a day for 19 days. The 19 days quickly became 18 and then 17 and, eventually, you had to pull a couple of all-nighters in order to pass the exam.

Some people of necessity must start later than others. I remember my father coming to me for advice when he was around 55. My sister had just gone out on her own and my parents were "empty nesters", at long last. My father told me that he had no savings. I recommended that he put the maximum allowable amount into a retirement plan and that he should try to keep working for as long as he could. He continued to work until he was 72. My parents were never big spenders and their vacations consisted of a month each year in Florida. My father died at the age of 92 and left a substantial estate.

Implementing a financial plan

In order for a person to set a goal, **the end result must be attainable**. One doesn't require a guarantee of success, but there has to be a reasonable chance. Thousands of boys play baseball and some who have more talent and drive set their goal towards become major leaguers. Not many get there. If you were age 40 and in good health and I were to offer you $10,000 to complete a 26 mile marathon in nine hours (a walking pace of three miles an hour), you might very well take me up on my offer. You know you'd be tired and sore at the end, but the challenge (and the money) would likely be worth it. On the other hand, if I offered you $1Million to run a marathon in less than 2 ½ hours, you'd laugh. There are only a handful of elite runners who can do this. As I said, to accept a challenge, there has to be some possibility of success.

Earlier, in this book, I told you that one can make numbers say virtually anything at all. Many people have the basic math skills to do the following:

Assumed age of a person today, married with 2 children
30
Assumed salary income today $40,000
Assumed average inflation rate for the next 35 years   4%

Calculated final earnings if pay raises equal inflation
$157,840 ($40,000x 3.946)
Assumed life expectancy from age 65 in years to age 82
17 years
Capital required at age 65 to produce an annual income of
around $160,000 for 17 years (4% yield) $1,946,560*
*($160,000x 12.166)

If I were to tell any 30-year-old person who earns $40,000 that he or she would need almost $2 Million to retire comfortably at age 65, I would be doing that person a great **disservice**. To set a goal that high would certainly appear unattainable. In fact that person would likely become so frustrated that he or she would conclude that it is probably best to forget about the future and live only for the present. Any inclination towards social responsibility- the need to provide for oneself- would evaporate.

This **"capital needs"** model based on the above figures is depicted in Exhibit 1 on the last page of this chapter. **It fails to take into account *normal life-cycle events* including, paying off one's home mortgage, children becoming independent, possible downsizing of the family home and reduced costs of travel and clothing with advanced age.**

Exhibit 2 reflects a much more accurate picture. It doesn't matter whether the graph is drawn to scale. For most people, the capital needed to fund a comfortable retirement is definitely attainable.

Remember that the "4 I's" tend to move in the same

direction. If inflation is high, incomes will tend to rise proportionately, as will interest and general investment yields.

My strong suggestion is that you *refrain from concentrating on the destination and focus on the journey.* If you are in your 30s or 40s and can set aside 10% of your family income each year to accelerate paying off your mortgage and then invest in an IRA and (if your future income permits) other investments, the destination will be very rewarding.

Life insurance

What I am doing in this chapter is outlining a "crash course" in financial planning. *I won't discuss the importance of having a will,* but I would be remiss if I didn't say at least a few words about life insurance. Building a nest egg takes time and perseverance. Moreover, it is crucial for you to protect yourself along the way, especially if you have dependents. Today, most families have two breadwinners. If one of them dies prematurely, leaving behind young children, the deceased person's income stream must be protected.

The answer for most people is low-cost term insurance to age 65 that contains a "double indemnity" clause (i.e. the policy pays out double the coverage) in the event of accidental death. This insurance is very inexpensive because, statistically, very few people die before age 65. It is true, if you outlive your policy, you will have paid premiums without ever receiving any benefits.

But, then again, you insure your home against fire loss. Do you hope it will burn down so that you might collect?

There are other insurance products that, in the long run, will provide an attractive cash value at some future time. These are more expensive and are generally purchased by higher- income individuals. Life insurance is also required if you have a business partner and your financial arrangement is structured so that, on the death of a partner, the survivor is obligated to buy out the deceased person's share.

My best suggestion is that you use the services of a qualified insurance broker or agent, who is not contracted to sell only one company's products. Be sure the person you deal with provides you with comparative quotes from several major companies.

In all cases, life insurance payments on death are tax free, while premiums paid are generally not tax-deductible.

Implementing an investment program

Whether you will be investing in an IRA or outside of a tax-sheltered plan, you will need to decide on a strategy with which you are comfortable. I wish I could tell you to sock away your money into **Federal Government insured** bank certificates or deposits and avoid risk entirely. Unfortunately, current yields are just too low.

Unless you have personal expertise, you are probably best off investing in a mutual fund that owns a diverse portfolio to reduce your risk. There are funds that invest in bonds and funds that invest in stocks. There are precious metals funds, real estate funds, oil& gas funds and funds that invest in stock indices like the Dow Jones Industrial average or the S&P 500. There are funds that invest in stocks and bonds of foreign entities. Each fund tries to attain a certain yield.

Generally, the higher the yield, the greater the risk. If you are willing to take a bit of time, there is a wealth of material on the Internet that might help you pinpoint the type of investments with which you would be comfortable. I suggest that you stick with mutual fund companies and managers that have been around long enough to develop acceptable "track records". Take a close look at their performance, not only in the "good" years, but also the "bad" ones, like 2008 and 2009. Be cautious with reference to anyone who offers an exceptional yield. Often, if it's too good to be true, it isn't!

In selecting an advisor, I believe your best bet is to get some referrals from people you trust, who are already reasonably wealthy and are either experienced investors or have benefited from good independent investment advice.

Here's to a bright future for all of us!

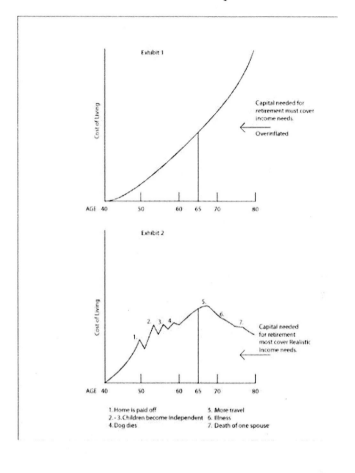

Exhibit 1

Cost of Living

Capital needed for
retirement must cover
income needs.

Overinflated

AGE 40   50   60   65   70   80

Exhibit 2

Cost of Living

5.

2. 3. 4.

1.

6.

7.

Capital needed
for retirement
most cover Realistic
income needs.

AGE 40   50   60   65   70   80

1. Home is paid off   5. More travel
2. - 3. Children become independent   6. Illness
4. Dog dies   7. Death of one spouse

EPILOGUE
SOME FINAL THOUGHTS ON POLITICAL REFORM

Politically, our country is sadly polarized. In the last Presidential election, Barack Obama became the first President since Dwight D. Eisenhower to win 51% of the votes *twice*. Mr. Obama garnered 65.9 Million votes, or 51.1%, while Mitt Romney's tally was 60.9 Million votes. *President Obama won the popular vote in only 26 states.*

I am not an expert on the question of why Americans vote for one person as opposed to another. Some may vote for the candidate that they feel is the more qualified. Others may be drawn by a particular candidate's charisma.

Another possibility is that a candidate might win an election by appealing to certain voter blocs. Yet, although Mr. Obama presumably benefited in the last two elections by attracting the African-American vote, there were also presumably large numbers of people who voted against him because they are (sadly) racially prejudiced. There is talk that the next Presidential election could feature a match between former First Lady and Senator Hillary Clinton and

Florida Senator Marco Rubio. It's an open question how many people would vote for or against Clinton because she is a woman and how many people would vote for or against Rubio because he is of Hispanic descent.

Overall, I believe that most *people vote the party and not the person.*

I suggest that it is often a candidate's position on a *single contentious issue* that will cause a person to vote for one party or the other. For example, Republicans are seen to be pro-life, while Democrats are seen as pro-choice. Democrats seem to favor gun control, while most members of the NRA (National Rifle Association) are Republicans

In Chapter 10, I suggested that the only way to deal with these contentious issues is to remove them from the table **permanently** through nation-wide referendums. If this is done, we, as a country, can focus on job creation, education reform and stamping out corruption in banking, investment markets and government. **These are the major issues.**

Honestly, I can't see *either* the Democrats or the Republicans as equal to the task of providing effective government, although I'd be happy to be proven wrong. I believe that meaningful changes will never be accomplished from the "top down."

What I believe is needed, is a new **grass-roots movement dedicated to a platform that can be presented to the American people clearly and succinctly.** *This* *grass roots movement must conquer voter apathy and must offer real hope for a better future by embracing the doctrine of Enlightened Capitalism.*

We must clean up our own house before we try to take on the entire Global Village and before we embark on the necessary steps to conquer worldwide poverty and to preserve our fragile environment.

I may be naïve, but I don't think it would cost billions of dollars for a new and vital political party to achieve recognition. The media is tired of "same old, same old" and the World Wide Web is readily available to disseminate The Doctrine of Enlightened Capitalism.

All that is needed is one leader and 535 other Americans across the country who would be willing to throw their hats into the ring and vie for 435 House seats and 100 seats in the U.S. Senate. These people must be ready to work in exchange for their salaries only and must be willing to ignore the efforts of lobbyists and special interest groups that are out to buy their votes

I recommend that this party be named **The New Federalist Party** to commemorate the first political party that was formed in America by Alexander Hamilton at the beginning of the 1790s. Mr. Hamilton envisioned **a strong national government with financial credibility. That is what we need more than ever today.**

Perhaps the first step is for us to decide on a direction that the U.S. should be following so that we may retain the pre-eminent status among nations that we are in serious danger of forfeiting.

The poll that follows is a good starting point. Please take the time to make your views known. Feel free to present your own thoughts and ideas.

I hope you have found this book informative and thought provoking.

Henry B. Zimmer

Big Bear Lake, California

August 2013

POLL INSTRUCTIONS

To print the entire poll, go to:
www.enlightenedcapitalism.us
and select the tab "The Enlightened Capitalism Poll (PDF Download)

To enter your responses, go to *www.enlightenedcapitalism.u*s and select the tab "The Enlightened Capitalism Poll". You do not have to answer every question.

The password to access the poll is: **enlightenedcapitalism**. (Not case sensitive.)

After you "Submit", your responses you will be directed to a tab called "View Cumulative Poll Results"

The password to view the up-to-date poll results at any time is **socialresponsibility** (Not case sensitive.)

You may submit/view comments at any time by going to the tab called "Comments"

The password to submit/view comments is **revitalizedamerica** (Not case sensitive.)

Please select the question number (using a three digit format) (e.g. "Question 007", "Question 043", "Question 113") and type in your comment.

Comments appear on the website in chronological order.

The webmaster reserves the right to reject comments that are not on topic, are not informative or are in bad taste.

THE ENLIGHTENED CAPITALISM POLL

Question 1: **Do you believe our top priority as Americans is to clean up our own economic and political house?**

Yes___ No____ Undecided___

Question 2: **Do you agree that <u>Unbridled</u> Capitalism must be stopped before our society collapses and that the self-interests of our nation's Capitalists, present and future, must be tempered with *social responsibility*?**

Yes___ No___ Undecided___

Question 3: **Do you understand that advocating Enlightened Capitalism is in no way the same as embracing Communism?**

Yes___ No___ Undecided___

Question 4: **Should all elections to the House of Representatives and the Senate be held at four-year intervals?**

Yes___ No___ Undecided___

Question 5: **Should the leader of the party with the most seats in the House of Representatives automatically become President of the United States?**

Yes___ No___ Undecided___

Question 6: **Should the respective roles of the House of Representatives and the Senate be redefined to eliminate overlap?**

Yes___ No___ Undecided___

Question 7: **Should the House of Representatives be primarily responsible for budgetary decisions and for domestic matters concerning the individual states?**

Yes___ No___ Undecided___

Question 8: **Should the Senate be primarily responsible for matters affecting the security of the Nation as a whole including international relations?**

Yes___ No___ Undecided___

Question 9: **Should lobbying by special interest groups be closely regulated to make it illegal to offer rewards in exchange for votes?**

Yes___ No___ Undecided___

Question 10: **Should campaign-financing rules be established that require National Parties, and not the Federal candidates themselves, to decide how funds are deployed?**

Yes___ No___ Undecided___

Question 11: **Should campaign spending restrictions be imposed for each Federal candidate?**

Yes___ No___ Undecided___

Question 12: **Do you support the concept of annual audits of the financial affairs of Members of Congress and their immediate families designed to expose irregularities?**

Yes___ No___ Undecided___

Question 13: **Do you support the concept of the annual audits suggested in Question 12 being extended until five years have elapsed after a Congressperson leaves office?**

Yes___ No___ Undecided

Question 14: **Do you support the administration of polygraph (lie detector) tests designed to detect bribes to Congresspersons and illegal acts?**

Yes___ No___ Undecided___

Question 15: **Do you support independent nation-wide referendums on contentious issues designed to obtain a consensus of public opinion?**

Yes___ No___ Undecided___

Question 16: **Do you agree that untaxed foreign profits of American companies should be taxed at regular corporate tax rates, unless they are repatriated and used to acquire or construct plants and equipment in the U.S. and/or are used to pay wages and benefits to new employees?**

Yes___ No___ Undecided___

Question 17: **Do you agree that our government and private industry should sponsor an ongoing campaign to convince consumers to buy products made in North America?**

Yes___ No___ Undecided___

Question 18: **Do you agree that basic executive remuneration should be capped by legislation and that additional compensation should be allowed only if each employee who has been with the company for at least two years receives a bonus of at least 5% of the average additional remuneration paid out to all executives who will earn in excess of the maximum base remuneration?**

Yes___ No___ Undecided___

Question 19: **Should the basic executive remuneration of senior executives be capped at $1.5 Million (in today's dollars)?**

Yes___ No. It should be higher___

No. It should be lower___ Undecided___

Question 20: **Do you think executive retirement payments and termination ("Golden Parachute") payments resulting from buy-outs should be limited to three times average remuneration for the previous three years?**

Yes___ No___ Undecided___

Question 21: **Do you agree that the maximum Federal tax on earned income should not exceed 33.3% to provide reasonable incentives for innovation and leadership?**

Yes___ No___ Undecided____

Question 22: **Do you agree that, if management shared remuneration equitably with employees, there would be little need for unions in the private sector, except to handle employee grievances?**

Yes___ No___ Undecided___

Question 23: **Do you agree that steps should be taken to reduce unemployment by having the government fund infrastructure development and redevelopment, including roads, bridges and highways?**

Yes___ No___ Undecided___

Question 24: **Do you agree that the military should be given the task of hiring and training employees to work on infrastructure projects and that Gulf war veterans should be given preference to fill supervisory positions?**

Yes___ No___ Undecided___

Question 25: **Do you agree that the U.S. should institute a peacetime draft under which young people, who are not in school, already working or incapacitated, should be required to participate for a three-year period for the purpose of carrying out infrastructure development and redevelopment projects? (No person drafted under this proposal would be required to engage in any military activities or combat outside of American soil unless they volunteer.)**

Yes___ No___ Undecided___

Question 26: **Do you agree that the activities of inductees should be divided between infrastructure-based assignments and educational pursuits that are tailored to each individual's interests and aptitudes?**

Yes___ No___ Undecided___

Question 27: **Do you agree that anyone who is required to participate in the draft but refuses should be prohibited from receiving any government handouts?**

Yes___ No___ Undecided___

Question 28: **Do you agree that anyone who is not a senior or handicapped and is dependent on government handouts should be required to provide support services to the infrastructure projects, each in accordance with their capabilities?**

Yes___ No___ Undecided___

Question 29: **Do you support President Obama's proposal to give 12 Million illegal immigrants amnesty and a path to citizenship?**

Yes___ No___ Undecided___

Question 30: Do you agree that the issue of amnesty for illegal immigrants should be decided by a nation-wide referendum?

Yes___ No___ Undecided___

Question 31: Do you agree that illegals should not be allowed to work in the U.S.?

Yes___ No___ Undecided___

Question 32: Do you believe that anyone who knowingly employs an illegal should be heavily fined?

Yes___ No___ Undecided___

Question 33: Do you agree that children born in the U.S. to illegal immigrants should be denied U.S. citizenship?

Yes___ No___ Undecided___

Question 34: Do you agree that the children of illegal aliens should be denied admission to U.S schools?

Yes___ No___ Undecided___

Question 35: **Do you agree that short selling of shares, bonds and other financial instruments traded on U.S. markets should be made illegal?**

Yes___ No___ Undecided

Question 36: **Do you agree that U.S. Exchange Traded Funds (ETFs) be prohibited from short selling of investments and/or markets?**

Yes___ No___ Undecided___

Question 37: **Do you agree that financial institutions (both publicly and privately owned) be assessed a 10% surtax on profits from day trading?**

Yes___ No___ Undecided___

Question 38: **Do you support the establishment of a legal concept called a "commodities interest" that would prohibit *anyone who is not in the business* of either producing or using a particular commodity (except gold and silver) from trading in it?**

Yes___ No___ Undecided___

Question 39: **Do you agree selling gold and silver be prohibited unless the seller is disposing of gold or silver that is already owned?**

Yes___ No___ Undecided___

Question 40: **Do you agree that buying "put" options should be made illegal unless the buyer owns the underlying investment and is using the put as an insurance policy against possible declines in value?**

Yes___ No___ Undecided___

Question 41: **Do you agree that senior executives of public companies be required to take polygraph (lie detector) tests quarterly before financial information is released in order to minimize fraud risk?**

Yes___ No___ Undecided___

Question 42: **Do you agree that businesses should be required to reflect property, plant and equipment at fair market values on their financial statements, such values to be determined by qualified independent appraisers?**

Yes___ No___ Undecided___

Question 43: **Do you agree that annual depreciation of property, plant and equipment should be determined by qualified independent appraisers, taking into account industry norms, when appropriate to do so?**

Yes___ No___ Undecided___

Question 44: **Do you agree that pension plans should be required to calculate over or under funding annually with reference to *current* investment yield rates instead of 25-year averages?**

Yes___ No___ Undecided___

Question 45: **Do you agree that all pension plans should be wound up with assets being distributed (without taxation before eventual withdrawal) to Individual Retirement Accounts (IRAs) of retirees and employees in an equitable manner with reference to current ages?**

Yes___ No___ Undecided___

Question 46: **Do you agree that, instead of having pension plans, employers should contribute annually to the personal IRAs of employees?**

Yes___ No___ Undecided___

Question 47: **Do you agree that a mandatory annual employer IRA contribution of 8% of salaries and wages to a maximum of $10,000 appears reasonable as a starting point?**

Yes___ No___ Undecided___

Questions 48-50 should be considered together:

Question 48: **Do you agree that employees should be permitted to match employer contributions to an IRA in whole or in part? (Employees may split their contributions between a regular and a Roth IRA.)**

Yes___ No___ Undecided___

Question 49: *In addition to the available tax deduction* **for regular IRA contributions, do you agree with the proposal that a 25% tax credit also be allowed, in order to reduce the average employee's after-tax cost of contributing to about 50% of total contributions?**

Yes___ No___ Undecided___

Question 50: **Do you agree that the "use it or lose it rules" should be repealed and that any eligible amount not contributed by an employee to an IRA in a given year should be available for an unlimited carry forward to any subsequent year?**

Yes___ No___ Undecided___

Question 51: **Do you agree that The Internal Revenue Code should be amended to restrict the deductibility of home mortgage interest (and property taxes) to these costs incurred with respect to ONE owner-occupied home?**

Yes___ No____ Undecided____

Question 52: **Do you agree that The maximum debt that qualifies for interest deductibility should be limited to THREE TIMES the adjusted gross income of the person or persons (in case a joint return is filed) who are claiming the deduction?**

Yes_____ No___ Undecided____

Question 53: **Do you agree that the maximum qualified debt limit on which interest is tax-deductible should be reduced from $1 million to $500,000?**

Yes___ No___ Undecided____

Question 54: **Do you agree that that the deductibility of interest on a Home Equity Line of Credit (HELOC) be restricted to situations where the loan proceeds are used for *structural home additions and improvements*?**

Yes___ No___ Undecided____

Question 55: **Do you agree that, to qualify for home mortgage interest deductibility, mortgage terms should be limited to *fifteen years*, and, if a home mortgage is refinanced, to retain deductibility, the maximum term of the refinancing should be limited to fifteen years minus the term that has elapsed since the initial mortgage financing was granted?**

Yes___ No__ Undecided_____

Question 56: **Do you agree that, in cases where people are "upside down" on their mortgages, they should be allowed to remain in their homes subject to the following conditions:**

- **They should be offered 15 year fixed financing at an interest rate of 5% on a principal amount of 75% of the amount owing to the institution that holds the particular mortgage.**
- **The remaining debt should be *deferred without interest for up to fifteen years.* If the homeowner and/or his immediate family are still living in the home at that time, this debt should then be *forgiven* (without any adverse income tax consequences).**
- **In the event that the home is sold before the fifteen-year period elapses, the deferred 25% amount of the original debt should be come due and payable, along with the outstanding balance of the 75% refinancing?**

Yes___ No___ Undecided____

Question 57: **Do you agree that, in cases where foreclosed homes are empty, prospective purchasers should be offered incentives to buy them and, to ensure that buyers act in good faith, they should be required** to make a down payment of 10% of the outstanding debt owing on the property; the lender would then provide fifteen-year fixed financing at 5% for 75% of the outstanding debt and *the remaining 15% would be deferred and forgiven in equal annual installments of one-fifteenth each year?*

Yes___ No___ Undecided___

Question 58: **Do you agree that Obamacare should be repealed?**

Yes___ No___ Undecided___

Question 59: **Do you agree that adopting a system of socialized medicine does not equate to embracing Communism?**

Yes___ No___ undecided___

Question 60: **Do you agree that concerns about potential patient satisfaction should be deferred until actual results are in- no matter what healthcare system is adopted?**

Yes___ No___ Undecided

Question 61: **Do you agree that a cost- effective healthcare system cannot exist if profit-oriented insurance companies administer it?**

Yes___ No___ Undecided___

Question 62: **Do you agree that, for a healthcare system to be effective, malpractice claims and awards should be regulated to protect physicians and reduce costs that are passed on to patients?**

Yes___ No___ Undecided___

Question 63: **Do you agree that a healthcare system should not erode our employment base by encouraging employers to outsource work and/or hire part-timers?**

Yes___ No___ Undecided___

Question 64: **Do you agree that, *IF a socialized healthcare program is adopted* a nominal charge ($20) would be appropriate in cases where a person visits a physician more than twice in a thirty-day period for routine treatment of the same malady?**

Yes___ No___ Undecided___

Question 65: **Please answer ONLY IF YOU ARE A NON-SMOKER. Do you agree that smokers should pay higher costs than non-smokers if socialized healthcare is adopted?**

Yes___ No___ Undecided___

Question 66: **Please answer ONLY IF YOU ARE A SMOKER. Do you agree that smokers should pay higher costs than non-smokers if socialized healthcare is adopted?**

Yes___ No___ Undecided___

Question 67: **Do you agree that pharmaceutical companies should not direct advertising towards consumers?**

Yes___ No___ Undecided___

Question 68: **Do you agree that, if a socialized healthcare system is adopted, the government should regulate prescription prices?**

Yes___ No__ Undecided___

Question 69: **Do you agree that, if a socialized healthcare system is adopted, the government should negotiate fees charged by *privately-owned* hospitals so that they may earn a reasonable rate of return on invested capital?**

Yes___ No___ Undecided___

Question70: **Do you agree that, if a socialized healthcare system is adopted, reasonable fitness center membership fees should be included as part of the coverage program, subject to reasonable minimum usage requirements?**

Yes___ No___ Undecided___

Question 71: **Do you agree that, if a socialized healthcare system is adopted, seniors should be included in the overall program as long as their cost is less than average amounts paid under the current system?**

Yes___ No___ Undecided___

Do you agree that, if a socialized healthcare system is adopted, seniors should receive the following benefits that they do not currently receive?

Question 72: **50% of routine dental work (not covered by the general healthcare system) up to $2,000 per annum.**

Question 73: **Hearing aid costs of up to $3,500 every two years.**

Question 74: **A daily subsidy for *basic* nursing home care that takes into account one's ability to pay.**

Question 75: **50% of prescription costs?**

Question 72   Yes___ No___ Undecided___

Question 73   Yes___ No___ Undecided___

Question 74   Yes___ No___ Undecided___

Question 75   Yes___ No___ Undecided___

Question 76: **Do you agree that estate and gift taxes should be repealed and replaced with deemed disposition rules to:**

1. trigger capital gains at the time growth property is gifted to anyone other than a spouse,
2. trigger a deemed sale at market value of growth property at the time of death, unless property is left to a spouse (or a trust where the spouse receives all the income as long as (s)he lives)?

(In all cases of *non-spousal* transfers, the recipient's

cost for tax purposes would become an amount equal to the deemed proceeds to prevent the same gain from being taxed twice.)

Yes___ No___ Undecided___

Question 77: **Do you agree that the maximum federal tax on earned income should be 33.3%?**

Yes___ No___ Undecided___

Question 78: **Do you agree that that the Internal Revenue Code be amended to simply exclude the first $1 Million of *lifetime gains* (or deemed gains) *of any individual* with respect to sales or transfers of small active-business corporations and family farms, as long as these have been held for 5 years or longer? (This would replace the far more complex provisions under present law.) If spouses owned a qualified business or farm jointly, the total exemption would become $2 Million.**

Yes___ No___ Undecided___

Question 79: **Do you agree that a small business corporate tax rate of 20% should apply to the first $250,000 of *annual active business earnings* of private corporations, as long as the after-tax profits are reinvested for business growth?**

Yes___ No___ Undecided___

Question 80: **Do you agree that the general corporate tax rate on active business income that does not qualify for the small business tax rate be set at 30%?**

Yes___ No___ Undecided___

Question 81: **Do you agree that the Subchapter S Corporation rules should be repealed as long as the corporate tax rates are reduced in accordance with the last two recommendations?**

Yes___ No___ Undecided___

Question 82: **Do you agree that dividends paid by private companies should only be subjected to a 10% tax in the hands of any individual recipient?**

Yes___ No___ Undecided___

Question 83: **Do you agree that the system of recording depreciation for income tax purposes should be simplified by reducing the number of asset categories and by adopting a single method for calculations?**

Yes___ No___ Undecided___

Question 84: **Do you agree that the rule requiring at least 80% ownership in order to transfer property to a corporation should be repealed and that the transferor should be allowed to recover his or her cost of the property without tax?**

Yes___ No___ Undecided___

Question 85: **Do you agree that the state and municipal tax-free bond rules should be amended to incorporate tax-free reciprocity between all the states?**

Yes___ No___ Undecided___

Question 86: **Do you agree that the alternative minimum tax provisions should be eliminated completely?**

Yes___ No___ Undecided___

Question 87: **Do you agree that the deduction for interest on money borrowed for investment purpose should be taken into account in determining adjusted gross income and not as an itemized deduction?**

Yes___ No___ Undecided___

Question 88: **Do you agree that the deduction for outside salesman expenses and unreimbursed employee expenses, including job training *and retraining,* should be taken into account in determining adjusted gross income and not as an itemized deduction?**

Yes___ No___ Undecided___

Question 89: **Do you agree that the deduction for job training expenses should be expanded to include job-*retraining* costs that would lead to potential *new* jobs?**

Yes___ No___ Undecided___

Question 90: **Do you agree that the tax rules for "claw backs" of deductions and credits otherwise available to higher income persons should be standardized in order to provide a common definition of what constitutes a "high –income person"?**

Yes___ No___ Undecided___

Question 91: **Do you agree that the child and dependent care credits should be restructured to reflect "real life" costs and that there should be no phase-out for higher income families?**

Yes___ No___ Undecided___

Question 92: **Do you agree that the deduction for tuition fees of up to $4,000, which is phased out for high-income taxpayers, should be eliminated and replaced by a modified Lifetime Learning credit of 25% of up to $10,000 per student per annum of post-secondary tuition fees and related costs?**

Yes___ No___ Undecided___

Question 93: **Do you agree that eligible educational institutions should include post-secondary vocational schools that award diplomas upon successful completion of studies?**

Yes___ No___ Undecided___

Question 94: Do you agree that the deduction for interest on educational loans of up to $2,500 per annum, which is phased out for high income taxpayers, should be replaced by a 25% credit on up to $4,000 of interest?

Yes___ No___ Undecided___

Question 95: Do you agree that tax-deductible contributions to Coverdell Education Savings Accounts (also referred to as Education IRAs) that are currently phased out for high-income persons, should be replaced by a 25% tax credit on contributions of up to $4,000 a year?

Yes___ No___ Undecided___

Question 96: Do you agree that the credit should only apply to savings for post-secondary education and not to defray the costs of private or prep schools for younger children?

Yes___ No___ Undecided___

Question 97: Do you agree that the deduction for personal exemptions that is phased out for higher-income taxpayers should be replaced by a 25% tax credit so that all Americans will be treated equally?

Yes___ No___ Undecided___

Question 98: **Do you agree that children should be tested in their early teens to determine their diverse aptitudes and interests and that they should then be streamlined into suitable educational and/or other programs designed for them to succeed?**

Yes___ No___ Undecided___

Question 99: **Do you agree that young people with the requisite interests and skill sets should be placed into apprenticeships and work-study programs that provide "real life" experience and prepare them for long-term suitable jobs and careers?**

Yes___ No___ Undecided___

Question 100: **Do you believe that the United States government should impose trading sanctions on countries that refuse to make a concerted effort to become more environmentally friendly?**

Yes___ No___ Undecided___

Question 101: **Do you agree that ground warfare is largely obsolete?**

Yes___ No___ Undecided___

Question 102: **Do you agree that military spending budgets should be cut where reasonably possible, with a major portion of the savings allocated to fund both the training of young people as well as implementing a workable healthcare system?**

Yes____ No____ Undecided____

Question 103: **Do you agree that the United States government should establish a general class of prohibited weapons that includes full automatics and other firearms more likely than not to be used primarily to assist in committing crimes?**

Yes____ No____ Undecided____

Question 104: **Do you believe that a binding nation-wide referendum should be held on the issue of gun control?**

Yes____ No____ Undecided____

Question 105: **Do you agree that we must practice religious tolerance in the United States and refrain from making any unwelcome attempts to coerce others to follow specific religious beliefs?**

Yes____ No____ Undecided____

Question 106: **Do you agree that there should be a nation-wide binding referendum on the issue of gay marriage and on the right of gays and lesbians to raise children?**

Yes___ No___ Undecided___

Question 107: **Are you totally against legalizing abortions under any circumstances?**

Yes___ No___ Undecided___

Question 108**: Would you support legalized abortion if the prospective mother's life or long-term health were at risk?**

Yes___ No___ Undecided___

Question 109: **Would you support legalized abortion if medical testing reveals mental or physical deformities in the unborn child?**

Yes___ No___ Undecided___

Question 110**: Do you believe that every woman is entitled to decide whether or not she wishes to bear a child?**

Yes___ No___ Undecided___

Question 111: **Should the death penalty be completely abolished?**

Yes___ No___ Undecided___

Question 112: **Should the death penalty apply as a possible sentence when someone is convicted of murdering a police officer or public official?**

Yes___ No___ Undecided___

Question 113: **Should the death penalty apply as a possible sentence when someone is convicted of mass murder?**

Yes___ No___ Undecided___

Question 114: **If the death penalty is accepted by referendum, should the sentence be carried out within 24 months?**

Yes___ No___ Undecided___

The Enlightened Capitalism Poll

In Memory of Jesus